Contents

Chapter 1: Business today

Business statistics	1
Big opportunities for small firms: government set to spend £1 in every £3 with small businesses	3
Growing pains for UK SMEs	4
Only China beats UK for rise in start-ups	5
Graduate entrepreneurs call for more support from universities	6
Why universities are the best places to start a business	7
Enterprise for all: the relevance of enterprise in education	8
The Tenner Challenge	10
Time to roll out real-world business studies?	12
"Work till you drop" warning on pensions	14
Crowded out: how crowdsourcing for start-ups turned into business as usual	15
Top 20: Britain's oldest family businesses	17
Why family business is big business	18
Understanding motivations for entrepreneurship	20
Supporting ethnic minority and female entrepreneurs	21
Revealed: how we're rebranding poor people as entrepreneurs	22

Chapter 2: Corporate responsibility

Corporate scandals and how (not) to handle them	23
As companies embrace the circular economy, are they missing a trick?	24
Is Chinese investment into the UK at record levels?	26
Tesco delayed payments to suppliers to boost profits, watchdog finds	27
Supermarkets: is it the end of an empire?	29
New guides for business owners in the dark over competition law	31
Corruption remains a major cost for honest companies	32
Half of UK banknotes used to fund shadow economy	33
Taxi-hailing service Uber paid just £22,134 corporation tax in UK	34
New criminal offences in clampdown on tax evasion	35
Share more profit with your workers, Centre for Social Justice tells big business	36
What is the new national living wage? How the April 2016 change could affect you	37
Ethics at work	39
Key facts	40
Glossary	41
Assignments	42
Index	43
Acknowledgements	44

Introduction

Business and Trade is Volume 298 in the **ISSUES** series. The aim of the series is to offer current, diverse information about important issues in our world, from a UK perspective.

ABOUT BUSINESS AND TRADE

The landscape of business and trade in the UK is constantly changing. This book explores current statistics, opportunities for small businesses and the outlook for graduates who wish to become self-employed. It also looks at business education, asking whether it is effective and relevant enough in the current economic climate. New ventures such as crowd funding are also considered, alongside the benefits of family-run businesses. And, finally, the second chapter looks at corporate responsibility – from tax scandals to ethics in the workplace.

OUR SOURCES

Titles in the **ISSUES** series are designed to function as educational resource books, providing a balanced overview of a specific subject.

The information in our books is comprised of facts, articles and opinions from many different sources, including:

⇨ Newspaper reports and opinion pieces

⇨ Website factsheets

⇨ Magazine and journal articles

⇨ Statistics and surveys

⇨ Government reports

⇨ Literature from special interest groups.

A NOTE ON CRITICAL EVALUATION

Because the information reprinted here is from a number of different sources, readers should bear in mind the origin of the text and whether the source is likely to have a particular bias when presenting information (or when conducting their research). It is hoped that, as you read about the many aspects of the issues explored in this book, you will critically evaluate the information presented.

It is important that you decide whether you are being presented with facts or opinions. Does the writer give a biased or unbiased report? If an opinion is being expressed, do you agree with the writer? Is there potential bias to the 'facts' or statistics behind an article?

ASSIGNMENTS

In the back of this book, you will find a selection of assignments designed to help you engage with the articles you have been reading and to explore your own opinions. Some tasks will take longer than others and there is a mixture of design, writing and research-based activities that you can complete alone or in a group.

FURTHER RESEARCH

At the end of each article we have listed its source and a website that you can visit if you would like to conduct your own research. Please remember to critically evaluate any sources that you consult and consider whether the information you are viewing is accurate and unbiased.

Useful weblinks

www.2degreesnetwork.com

www.bmmagazine.co.uk

www.centreforsocialjustice.org.uk

www.channel4.com

www.controlrisks.com

www.theconversation.com

www.enterprisenation.com

www.esrc.ac.uk

www.familybusinessunited.com

www.fullfact.org

www.gov.uk

www.theguardian.com

www.heraldscotland.com

www.huffingtonpost.co.uk

www.ibe.org.uk

www.policybee.co.uk

researchbriefings.parliament.uk/

www.rsagroup.com

www.sustainablefoodtrust.org

www.telegraph.co.uk

www.tenner.org.uk

www.young-enterprise.org.uk

Bu

Independence Educational Publishers

First published by Independence Educational Publishers

The Studio, High Green

Great Shelford

Cambridge CB22 5EG

England

Copyright

Photocopy licence

ISBN-13: 978 1 86168 739 5

Printed in Great Britain
Zenith Print Group

Business statistics

By Chris Rhodes

⇨ In 2015, there were 5.4 million businesses in the UK.

⇨ Over 99% of businesses are small or medium sized businesses – employing 0–249 people.

⇨ 5.1 million (95%) businesses were micro-businesses – employing 0-9 people. Micro-businesses accounted for 33% of employment and 18% of turnover.

⇨ In London, there were 1,434 businesses per 10,000 resident adults. In the North East there were 629 per 10,000 resident adults.

⇨ The service industries accounted for 74% of businesses, 79% of employment and 71% of turnover.

⇨ The manufacturing sector accounted for 5% of businesses, 10% of employment and 16% of turnover.

⇨ There were 351,000 business births and 246,000 business deaths in 2014.

⇨ 20% of SMEs (small and medium-sized enterprises) are female-led, and in October 2015 it was announced that 26% of FTSE100 board members were female.

Businesses in the UK

In 2015, there were 5.4 million private sector businesses in the UK, up by 146,000 or 3% since 2014.

Since 2000, the number of businesses in the UK has increased each year, by 3% on average. In 2015, there were 1.9 million more businesses than in 2000, an increase of 55% over the whole period.

The proportion of businesses that employ people has fallen since 2000 from around a third, to around a quarter. This decline in the number of employers as a proportion of all businesses is due to the growth in self-employment.

The number of sole proprietorships (businesses with no employees) has grown by more than the number of all businesses (by 73% compared to 55% for all businesses).

Businesses by size

The usual definition of small and medium-sized enterprises (SMEs) is any business with fewer than 250 employees. There were 5.4 million SMEs in the UK in 2015, which was over 99% of all businesses.

Micro-businesses have 0–9 employees. There were 5.1 million microbusinesses in the UK in 2015, accounting for 95% of all businesses.

Although the vast majority of businesses in the UK employ fewer than ten people, this sort of business only accounts for 33% of employment and 18% of turnover. Large businesses, with more than 250 employees, accounted for 0.1% of businesses but 40% of employment and 53% of turnover.

Businesses by region

In the UK in 2015 there were 1,028 businesses per 10,000 resident adults. In London there were 1,434 businesses per 10,000 residents, whilst in the North East there were 629 businesses per 10,000 residents.

A third of UK businesses are in London or the South East (976,000 in London and 878,000 in the South East). Northern Ireland has 117,000 businesses whilst the North East has 136,000.

The North East saw a 10% fall in the number of businesses last year, whilst the UK overall saw a 3% increase. The West Midlands, the East Midlands and Northern Ireland also saw falls in their business population.

Businesses by industry

In 2015 there were 4.0 million businesses in the service industries, three quarters of all businesses in the UK. The biggest of the service industries in terms of the number of businesses was the professional, scientific and technical industry which accounted for 15% of businesses. The retail sector accounted for 10% of all businesses.

Overall, businesses in the service industries accounted for 79% of employment and 71% of total turnover. Businesses in the retail sector alone accounted for 19% of employment and 37% of all turnover in 2015.

Construction sector businesses accounted for 18% of all businesses, but only 8% of employment and 7% of turnover. This is explained by the fact that a large number of construction workers are self-employed, boosting the number of enterprises, but not the number employed in the sector.

Manufacturing firms accounted for 5% of businesses, 10% of employment and 16% of turnover.

Business births and deaths

In 2014 in the UK, there were 351,000 business births, up 4,000 on the previous year. Business births outnumber business deaths by 105,000 in 2014, the second largest margin since the series began (the largest margin was in 2013).

2011 was the first year that the business birth rate was higher than the business death rate since 2008. In 2014, the business birth rate was 14%, whilst the business death rate was 10%.

Business births and deaths by region

In 2014, the largest number of business births occurred in London (89,000). The largest number of business deaths also occurred in London (53,000). In all the regions and countries of the UK, business births outnumbered business deaths.

The business death rate was broadly the same in all the regions of the UK – within a percentage point of 10%. There was more variation in the business birth rate: 9% in Northern Ireland compared with 18% in London. Most other regions had birth rates of around 14%.

Women in business

Various sources are used in this section to provide an indication of female involvement in business in the UK.

Female-led SMEs

In 2014, 20% of SMEs in the UK were majority led by women. This is two percentage points higher than in 2012 and equates to around 1.1 million SMEs.

Business at least partially led by women accounted for 38% of all SMEs in 2014, around 2.0 million SMEs.

Examining only SMEs with employees, women-led SMEs are underrepresented in the manufacturing and construction sectors (accounting for only 7% and 8% of business, respectively), but account for 43% of businesses in the combined public administration, education, health and defence sector.

It is estimated that in the UK women-led SME businesses contribute about £75 billion to economic output (16% of the UK SME approximate GVA total).[1]

Female start-ups

Estimates have been made of the proportion of women involved in 'total early stage entrepreneurial activity'

or TEA. TEA includes the owning or running of any business that is less than three and a half years old.[2]

In 2014, the TEA rate (the proportion of working-aged people involved in TEA) in the UK was 11%. By gender, the TEA rate in the UK was 8% among women and 14% among men.[3]

Using these data we can estimate that 35% of TEA in the UK was accounted for by women in 2014. In the US, 40% of TEA was accounted for by women.[4]

The same source can be used to compare female entrepreneurship in different countries. A positive gender gap means that the male TEA rate is higher than the female rate. A negative gender gap means that the female TEA rate is higher than the male TEA rate.

In the UK, the TEA gender gap was 6.3, above the rate in many of the UK's competitor countries, such as the US (5.3), France (2.7) and Germany (2.6).

Women on boards

A target that FTSE100 boards should have a minimum of 25% female representation by 2015 was set in the 2011 report by Lord Davies of Abersoch, Women on boards.[5]

In October 2015, it was announced that this target had been met, and that 26% of FTSE100 board members were female.

There are now zero all-male boards in the FTSE100, down from 21 in 2011. In the FTSE350, there are now 15 all-male boards, down from 152 in 2011.[6]

Lord Davies' report states that against his target, Unilver and Marks and Spencer were the best performing boards in October 2015, with female representation of 50% and 42% respectively.[7]

7 December 2015

⇨ The above information contains public sector information licensed under the Open Government Licence v3.0 and is reprinted from the House of Commons Library. Please visit researchbriefings. parliament.uk for further information.

© Crown copyright 2016

1 BIS, Small Business Survey 2012: businesses led by women and ethnic minorities, 2013, p 2. Output is Gross Value Added.

2 Global Entrepreneurship Monitoring Consortium, Global 2014 Monitoring Report, January 2015, p 12

3 Ibid, pp 36 and 86

4 These data assume that there is the same number of male and female people of working age.

5 Lord Davies of Abersoch and BIS, Women on boards, February 2011, p 4

6 Lord Davies of Abersoch and BIS, Five year summary report, October 2015, p 34

7 Ibid, p 13

Big opportunities for small firms: government set to spend £1 in every £3 with small businesses

We are setting an ambitious target that £1 in every £3 government spends will be with small businesses by 2020.

Matt Hancock, the Minister for the Cabinet Office has announced an ambitious new target to get more small businesses working on central government contracts.

In 2013 to 2014, central government spent an unprecedented £11.4 billion with small and medium-sized businesses – those employing 250 employees or less. This is equivalent to 26% of central government spend.

By 2020, the Government wants to increase this to a third. This would mean an extra £3 billion per year (in 2013 to 2014 terms) going to small and medium-sized firms directly or through the supply chain.

Earlier this year, the Government improved the way it buys goods and services to help more small businesses bid for public sector contracts, by:

⇨ requiring the entire public sector supply chain to be paid within 30 days

⇨ abolishing pre-qualification questionnaires for low value public sector contracts, making it simpler and quicker to buy

⇨ requiring the public sector to publish its contracts in one place on Contracts Finder.

Each government department and the Crown Commercial Service will now make sure that it meets this target by setting out individual plans and targets for spending with small and medium-sized businesses over the next five years.

Minister for the Cabinet Office, Matt Hancock said:

"This is such an amazing opportunity for the country's diverse and innovative small businesses, and today I urge them to get stuck in. From computers to uniforms – there are so many opportunities for small businesses to work with us, and I want to see more of them providing value for money for the taxpayer and benefiting from our spending."

John Allan, National Chairman for the Federation of Small Businesses (FSB), said:

"The Government has much to gain from opening up public procurement to smaller businesses and we welcome the Government's commitment to achieve this ambitious target. To meet it, the Government will need to focus on robust monitoring and challenge of poor practices wherever they are found. The FSB will play its part, and will work with ministers on this important goal."

John Manzoni, Chief Executive of the Civil Service said:

"Further opening up our marketplace to small businesses is good economic sense all round – making it easier for them to access and win government business opportunities, whilst encouraging increased competition and market innovation to deliver best value for the taxpayer."

27 August 2015

⇨ The above information is reprinted with kind permission from the Cabinet Office, The Rt Hon. Matt Hancock MP and Crown Commercial Service. Please visit www.gov.uk for further information.

Growing pains for UK SMEs

Micro-businesses flourish, as proportion of high-growth companies falls.

⇨ New generation of 'micropreneurs' changes landscape of UK business economy.

⇨ UK adds 1.4 million micro firms (up 43%) to business landscape since 2000.

⇨ Zero-employee firms[1] are the fastest-growing business size category since 2007, up 21.4 per cent.

⇨ The proportion of high-growth companies[2] fell by more than 20 per cent since 2005.

⇨ High-growth expected to recover, but businesses need more government support.

UK businesses are increasingly micro in size,[3] while the proportion of high-growth companies has fallen considerably in recent years, causing a drag on economic development potential, according to new research from RSA, the UK's largest commercial insurer. High-growth companies are defined as those achieving on average 20 per cent annual growth in employment for three consecutive years.

The new study, _Growing Pains_, which examines the shape of the UK business economy and the biggest barriers to achieving growth, is based on in-depth analysis of the latest economic data and opinion research among small business owners and managers. While the high proportion of SMEs in the UK is well documented, the research found that micro-sized businesses are the only size category to have grown their proportion of the UK business stock since 2000 – compared with small, medium and large-sized businesses – rising sharply by 1.4 million or 43 per cent.

What looks like an increase in entrepreneurship is actually a new generation of 'micropreneurs' or sole traders. When looking at more detailed size band information, the number of zero-employee firms has increased by 21.4 per cent since the

> **Small and medium-sized enterprises (SMEs) are made up of enterprises which employ fewer than 250 persons and which have an annual turnover not exceeding 50 million euro, and/or an annual balance sheet total not exceeding 43 million euro.**

recession, making this the fastest growing business size category analysed.

According to the study, turnover per worker climbs steadily in line with employee numbers, with companies employing 250–499 people yielding the highest turnover per employee (£186,100 on average). Therefore, helping more businesses to grow should reap greater economic benefit.

David Swigciski, SME Trading Director at RSA, comments: "The UK has long been regarded as a great place to start a business, but the recent recession has had a significant impact on the business economy, with companies becoming smaller in size. Unfortunately, continuing along this road isn't an option if we want a sustained recovery from the economic downturn.

"Getting back on track and strengthening the economic recovery is a case of redressing the balance between start-ups and growth. This can be done by encouraging investment in growth and helping – as well as ensuring – SMEs reach their full growth potential."

Growing pains

Since 2005, the share of firms that were classified as high-growth plummeted across all geographical regions except London. The decline was greatest in Wales, where the proportion of high-growth

businesses fell by more than half, and Scotland, where it was down by more than a third.

Worryingly, medium-sized firms were more likely to have become small (16.5%) than large (3.6%) between 2008 and the latest available records (2011), with 79.9 per cent remaining as medium in terms of their employee numbers.

Looking ahead to 2017, the number of high-growth enterprises is expected to recover as a result of improving economic conditions. However, the proportion of businesses that are classified as high-growth is expected to remain below 2005 levels in all regions except London, which will continue to outperform the rest of the UK.

The research found that two-thirds (64%) of small business owners describe themselves as ambitious, with large differences throughout the country. The most ambitious businesses are found in Wales (80%) while the least ambitious are based in Scotland (45%).

Despite this general optimism, a third (34%) of small business owners admit that it is getting harder, not easier, to grow against a backdrop of uncertainty around interest rates, and in the lead up to the 2015 General Election. Two-thirds (66%) say the Government must do more to de-risk business growth, rising to 80 per cent in London and the South East. A further three-quarters (73%) say the Government must make it easier for SMEs to access the right information and support for growth, rising to 84 per cent in the Midlands and 80 per cent in London and the South East.

Swigciski continues: "Our research shows that the number of high growth businesses is expected to recover, yet the proportion will remain below pre-crisis levels. This suggests that the Government's business growth package is focused on the right kinds of support, but this needs to be sustained and built upon further.

"Despite the Government's recent efforts, small businesses are still crying out for more support and better access to information. For instance, clear direction on where to turn to for advice and extending the current apprenticeship scheme could both have a significant impact."

Footnotes

1. Zero-employee firms are defined in this study as companies with no additional employees, other than the founder of the business. They are also described throughout the research as 'micropreneurs'.

2. 'High growth' businesses are defined as achieving an average 20 per cent annual growth in employment for three consecutive years. The high growth 'rate' is the number of those firms as a proportion of all firms with 10+ employees in the base year. Projections for 2011–14 and 2014–17 are based on Cebr's economic growth forecasts.

3. The firm size classes used in this research are Micro (0–9 employees), Small (10–49), Medium (50–249) and Large (250+).

23 September 2014

⇨ The above information is reprinted with kind permission from the RSA Insurance Group plc. Please visit www.rsagroup.com for further information.

Only China beats UK for rise in start-ups

Only China has seen stronger growth in the number of new businesses over the past five years, according to analysis of start-up numbers in 22 countries.

Accountancy group UHY Hacker Young said that since the depths of the global recession in 2010, the rate at which new businesses were established in the UK was the second highest out of the countries analysed.

Britain saw a 51% increase in new businesses from 385,741 in 2010 to 581,173 in 2014. This compares to an 11% increase in the US, 7% in Japan, 40% in Germany and 39% in France.

The study claimed that efforts by the UK Government to reduce taxes and reduce red tape helped boost start-up numbers, with the country now ranking as the number one nation in the G7 and sixth globally to launch and operate a business according to recent World Bank data.

An entrepreneur in the UK can now start a company in the UK in less than five days, compared to the global average of 20.

The report said strong growth in alternative finance providers such as peer-to-peer lending and crowdfunding has also helped encourage new British entrepreneurs.

Colin Jones, partner at UHY Hacker Young, said: "The UK is now a leading nation for start-ups and providing them with the right environment to grow.

"Although the economy has bounced back from the recession, the coming years will bring their own challenges, and governments around the world need to find ways to turn these new start-ups into prosperous businesses.

"The [UK] Government has simplified regulations and established a Start Up Loans programme, but it needs to maintain this strong level of assistance. There is always room for improvement in cutting red tape and making life easier for entrepreneurs and investors."

23 November 2015

⇨ The above information is reprinted with kind permission from Enterprise Nation. Please visit www.enterprisenation.com for further information.

Graduate entrepreneurs call for more support from universities

Are the UK's universities missing their students' entrepreneurial potential? According to graduates, they could be...

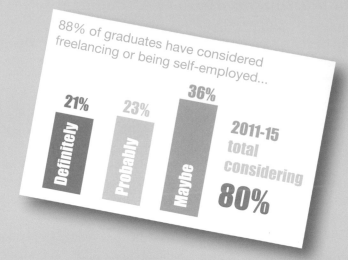

88% of graduates have considered freelancing or being self-employed...

21% Definitely
23% Probably
36% Maybe

2011-15 total considering **80%**

...with more men than women considering going it alone

48% **52%**

More than half of graduates freelanced during their studies...

...for these reasons

45% 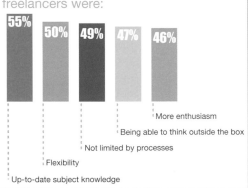 to gain experience

22% to help pay bills

Graduates thought the biggest barriers to going freelance were:

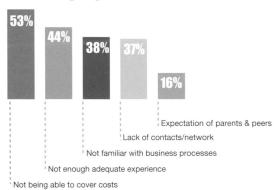

53%
44%
38%
37%
16%

Expectation of parents & peers
Lack of contacts/network
Not familiar with business processes
Not enough adequate experience
Not being able to cover costs

Graduates thought the biggest advantages of taking on graduate freelancers were:

55%
50%
49%
47%
46%

More enthusiasm
Being able to think outside the box
Not limited by processes
Flexibility
Up-to-date subject knowledge

Most graduates' universities didn't offer enough advice about freelancing and self-employment

62% Not discussed at all
19% Discussed but not in depth
12% Did discuss

Infographic reproduced with kind permission from PolicyBee. Please visit www.policybee.co.uk for further information.
© PolicyBee

Research was conducted by Youth Sight on behalf of PolicyBee during July 2015, among 1,002 graduates.

Why universities are the best places to start a business

THE CONVERSATION

An article from **The Conversation.**

By Steven West, Vice-Chancellor, University of the West of England

Creative ideas and how we turn them into successful business ventures and social enterprises are vital to the UK's global competitiveness. But how do we best support this?

Of course there are many different ways to start a business. But I strongly challenge those who say point blank that a university experience is a waste of time for future entrepreneurs, or that a degree is just a piece of paper. Yes, it is true that students only grow into 'experts' when they also learn in a practical environment, but the idea that they don't do this at university is not one I recognise. Students don't simply learn from a textbook within the walls of the classroom.

Modern ways of learning

Programmes are often co-designed with employers, and students can engage in exciting real world projects, such as the Bloodhound SSC collaboration project to break the land speed record.

Students also learn from simulation activities, which have real-time employer engagement and live projects on site such as the development of buildings or ground-breaking research projects. They also

have opportunities for placements and internships with industry leaders and innovative small businesses or workshops with practitioners at the cutting edge of their industry sectors.

Universities are now a hotbed for successful enterprise. The facts speak for themselves. In the 2012–13 academic year, universities and higher education institutions supported the creation of more than 3,500 start-ups by their recent graduates. This brought the total of active graduate companies created in the last 13 years to 8,127, employing 15,588 staff, receiving investments totalling £28.5 million and having a combined turnover in 2012–13 of £376 million.

Bricks and ideas

In my view there are three elements that make many of our universities the best place to start a business.

First are the connections and networks they provide. Universities are often at the heart of local economies. They are often uniquely placed to bring together users and experts to identify issues, generate solutions, and bring new services to market. They often act as the anchor that pulls people together – providing a focal point for interaction – as highlighted in the recent Witty report on encouraging a British invention revolution.

Universities often run innovation networks, work closely with Local Enterprise Partnerships in support of local economic growth, and provide a link for small businesses to other business support networks, such as the Growth Accelerator, UK Trade and Investment and the Manufacturing Advisory Service.

Second, universities also offer access to the facilities and expertise students need

to fully develop and test their ideas – such as with robotic technologies or laser printing. We know this is also highly valued by business, for example through working closely with funding bodies such as the Technology Strategy Board to help small businesses access funding through Knowledge Transfer Partnerships, which allow start-up, micro, small and medium-sized businesses to buy in expertise from universities, colleges and public sector research establishments.

Third, universities are leading a variety of high-impact enterprise initiatives for students, as showcased last year by the University Alliance, of which I am chair, and the National Association of College and University Entrepreneurs. We know universities need to be creative, with student competitions and funding, as well as enterprise internships.

We have taken this one step further with a BA Business (Team Entrepreneurship) at UWE Bristol – where students work in a high-tech hub rather than a classroom. They have coaching sessions and workshops rather than compulsory lectures – and it is running a real business that drives the students' learning.

Importantly, individuals are also encouraged to reflect on their experiences. We know business failure is much less likely to be seen as a learning opportunity by UK entrepreneurs: 13% thought so compared to the G20 average of 23%.

With reports of more than a fifth of new businesses failing within the first 12 months, it is critical that we see failure as a learning opportunity – in order to prevent it becoming a barrier.

Room for improvement

There are of course a number of issues to address as we work to support enterprise and nurture the entrepreneurial culture we need throughout the UK.

One question that arises for universities as some develop funds to provide financial support for start-ups, is the size of the financial stake it is appropriate for them to take in fledgling businesses. Of course, this is dependent on the level of investment put in – financial or facilities.

But as we go down this route, I would argue that we are best placed looking to models in the US where the aim is for universities to make lots of small investments by taking a 2–3% stake in the resulting companies. And this would be with a higher goal in mind – establishing a long-term relationship and generating future opportunities through engagement.

For government, one very pressing issue is to ensure that the highly successful Cambridge model – supporting start-ups and spin-outs from the so-called 'Silicon Fens' – is rolled out across the UK, from Bristol to Lincoln, Plymouth, Teeside and elsewhere. Cambridge is a great example of what can be achieved, but if that is the extent of our ambition, we are in trouble.

Starting and sustaining your own business is not easy. Universities don't just offer knowledge and skills on how to develop ideas, enter new markets and utilise digital technologies. They can also offer the connections, networks and support to help individuals flourish. There is no other place where budding entrepreneurs will have access to so many people to spark ideas off – to test them with their peers, experts and professionals.

7 May 2014

⇨ The above information is reprinted with kind permission from *The Conversation*. Please visit www.theconversation.com for further information.

Enterprise for all: the relevance of enterprise in education

The relevance of enterprise in education is Lord Young's third and final report on enterprise.

When the Internet reached critical mass it changed far more than the social and shopping habits of the nation. Only a few years ago the definition of a small firm was one employing fewer than 500: today 95.5% of firms by number in this country employ fewer than ten. The skills sought by large companies, invariably process-driven, were in those days typified by team sports and conformity and that is what the school system was encouraged to deliver. The world of those now leaving education will be one in which self-reliance and creativity will be rewarded and the education system will have to adapt. Nothing in this report will undermine the present curriculum; indeed the most employable skills of all are the three Rs – but they, by themselves, may not be sufficient unless accompanied by an enterprising attitude.

Enterprise means more than just the ability to become an entrepreneur. It is that quality that gives an individual a positive outlook, an ability to see the glass as half full rather than half empty, and is a valuable attribute for the whole of life. It is a quality many bring with them on starting primary school but far too many leave secondary school without. This report looks at fostering an enterprising attitude in both formal and informal education, including the desire to become an entrepreneur, and encouraging more to enter self-employment or start their own company.

It is not just the business world that has changed. We are now asking young people who leave the school system at 18 to make a serious economic decision when they choose a particular university and degree course. By making a Future Earnings and Employment Record available, as outlined in my report, we will enable them to decide if a particular course makes sense. I have spent enough years in the higher education sector to know how jealously universities regard their reputations and how they compare their results with their peers; the availability of this kind of information will be a powerful driver for raising standards throughout the sector.

It is now well over 30 years since I played a part in the introduction of the Youth Training Scheme. The challenges we faced then are similar to those we have today, namely, the number of young people who leave school demotivated with few or no qualifications. It is difficult for many young people to connect what they are asked to learn in school with the outside world and that is why I am proposing that head teachers have an Enterprise Adviser to assist them by introducing speakers from all walks of life to enthuse pupils in the classroom. We must also make many of the subjects learned in school more relevant to the outside world, including encouraging more pupils in STEM (Science, Technology, Engineering and Maths) subjects. I anticipate that the Local Enterprise Partnerships may well wish to have a coordinating role.

But people are more than just the sum of their qualifications. There are many activities in and around school that help to broaden the experience of the individual. We have introduced a programme called Fiver* which is giving primary school pupils £5 for the month of June to see what they can make of it and I look forward to meeting those that have done best after the summer. We have received 27,000 registrations for Fiver so far, far exceeding the 20,000 target for this first year, and we will be looking to double this programme over the next two years. There are many other activities that take place in and around schools. Quite apart from Outward Bound and other similar programmes, there are often school companies, work experience, additional vocational courses and enterprising summer and holiday activities. That is why I am proposing an Enterprise Passport that will follow an individual throughout their time in education. This passport will be digital, will list all the extramural and other activities and will, for example, enable an employer to take a more rounded view of that individual other than by assessing academic qualifications alone. I could see it being a useful adjunct in university entrance as well.

Teachers will have a key role to play if we are to support the learning of young people with the right mix of enterprise and employability skills. I have met many talented teachers up and down the country who are already demonstrating imaginative and enterprising approaches to teaching and learning, and I want to encourage them to go further to promote their pupils' enterprise capabilities. I have therefore proposed that all teachers be given the opportunity to spend a week with a large organisation, public or private, on a special course designed to bring out the skills and attitudes required in tomorrow's world. I also propose that facilities be made available to enable teachers to spend some of their inset days with employers.

We have many excellent further education colleges that produce hundreds of thousands of young people with highly employable skills, but my research has found that only a small number of college courses prepare their students for self-employment or setting up a business. In fact many graduates, be they plumbers, plasterers, hairdressers or many of the other skills acquired in a further education college, may well want to start working for themselves. That

is why I am recommending that all courses should include a core module on starting a business so that all graduates will leave with the necessary skills.

Last year we started working with university business schools and as a result many are now reaching out to small firms in their vicinity. Business schools have, up to now, devoted themselves to producing executives for large companies and, as a result of the steps we took last year, we will see more entrepreneurs coming from the schools themselves. However, within the whole body of students at any university, be they on courses as diverse as archaeology to zoology, individuals may wish to work for themselves or indeed go into business to help others, as the substantial growth of social enterprises in recent years can attest. The steps outlined in my report will enable many more entrepreneurs to emerge from the general body of students.

It is difficult to exaggerate the importance of enterprise in all its forms in a modern economy. This report outlines a number of steps we can take over the next few years but much more needs to be

done. I am reminded that many of the initiatives I introduced in the 1980s as a minister evolved into stronger programmes that were able to adapt over time, and I hope that the proposals I set out in this report can be seen as a foundation for us to build on. We can no longer afford to be an island in a globalised world and our competitors will not wait for us.

2014

⇨ The above information is reprinted with kind permission from the Department for Business, Innovation & Skills and Prime Minister's Office 10 Downing Street. Please visit www.gov.uk for further information.

© Crown copyright 2016

*Fiver is a Young Enterprise scheme and more details can be found at www.fiverchallenge.org.uk.

The Tenner Challenge

An extract from the Young Enterprise Evaluation Report, 2014/15.

The Tenner Challenge is a four-week UK-wide competition that challenges young people to take a £10 pledge, do something enterprising, make a difference and give back. This year, the Tenner Challenge[1] took place over the period 23 February–20 March.

Young people taking part in Tenner have the opportunity to set up their own mini business and take on all the challenges involved in setting up and running their own enterprise, from creating a product, designing a company logo, working as a team and managing a budget. Tenner also encourages social responsibility at a local level as many students set up projects with all or part of proceeds donated to local communities, schools or national charities.

Tenner 2015 in numbers

⇨ 432 UK centres registered

⇨ 20,673 participants registered

⇨ Average profit: £156

⇨ Top 50 teams: total profit of £32,500

⇨ 76% of teams donated all or part of their profits to charities for a total of £29,147 – the highest donation being £5,212

⇨ 87% of students would recommend Tenner to friends

⇨ 83% of students feel Tenner has provided them with an unique opportunity to learn and achieve new things

⇨ Average of two students per team

⇨ Average of 11 teams per school

⇨ Average age is 14

⇨ 65% of students wishing to take part in extra curricular activities outside schools following the Tenner Challenge

⇨ 90% of teachers agree that the Tenner Challenge has increased

1   Tenner is run by Young Enterprise and supported by BGF.

Young Enterprise Tenner Challenge: team activities

The Tenner Challenge is a four week UK-wide competition that challenges young people to take a £10 pledge, do something enterprising, make a difference and give back.

Legend:
- Creating a new product
- Organising events
- Selling a service
- Selling customised items
- Selling food
- Other

Pie chart values: 6%, 25%, 10%, 13%, 38%, 7%

Source: Young Enterprise Tenner Challenge: Evaluation Report, *Tenner, 2014/15*

young people's financial knowledge and understanding.

Who and where are the Tenner participants?

Young people

Based on the 20,673 registered students, Tenner was mostly endorsed in the South East, South West, North West, West Midlands and London. Together, these regions accounted for half of all students (64%).

Year groups

Upon completing their online registrations, teachers select the year groups they are engaging in the Tenner Challenge. Data shows that over a third (41%) teach Year 9 and Year 10, both approximately accounting for 20% of centres registered.

Employability skills development

The employability competency framework is the Young Enterprise in-house guiding framework that supports the Tenner Challenge evaluation process, capturing

young people's skills progression data across the following ten competencies:

1. Resilience

2. Adaptability

3. Problem solving

4. Teamwork – cooperation

5. Communication

6. Confidence

7. Organisation

8. Creativity

9. Teamwork – listening.

Participants were surveyed before and immediately after Tenner to identify changes in skills and intentions. Our test sample is composed of 1,331 students, belonging to 505 teams across 125 schools. Student's results were matched using unique individual and team identifiers, thereby enabling us to calculate differences in scores and link students to respective teams, schools and teachers.

Findings show an increase in mean scores pre- and post-Tenner across all competencies except for Teamwork – cooperation. The greatest progressions are in creativity, communication and confidence – all of which are statistically significant results at the 95% confidence level.

Furthermore:

⇨ 83% of participants feel that Tenner has provided them with an opportunity to learn and achieve new things.

⇨ 71% experienced a progression in between one to five competencies (on average young people experienced a progression across five competencies).

⇨ 58% feel that Tenner has helped them in further defining their career choices.

Entrepreneurial attitudes

Tenner evaluation also looks at key entrepreneurial attitudes. A series of three business oriented statements were presented to participants testing their preferences and attitudes towards self-employment:

1. I know what running my own business would involve.
2. Running my own business sounds like a good idea.
3. I am aware of self-employment as a career path.

All statements show a progression in average pre- and post- scores except for no. 2. This is a similar finding to our 2014 results in which feedback from young people and teachers attribute to the business realities that young people face when setting up and running their business. Undeniably, going through the process bring to the fore the steps and qualities required to set up businesses which many might find discouraging right after the Tenner Challenge; especially if the team made a loss.

Social outcomes

Part of the Tenner Challenge encompasses the notion of social responsibility by enabling participants to look at the '3 Ps': Profit, People they engage with and Planet.

⇨ 65% of young people agreed that Tenner helped in making their school and local community a nice place.

⇨ 76% of teams donated all or part of their profits to charities for a total of £29,147 – the highest donation being £5,212.

⇨ 65% of young people say that following Tenner, they will now take part in extra-curricular activities outside school.

This suggests that the Tenner Challenge encourages community engagement, both within school and the wider local area.

Conclusion

⇨ The Young Enterprise Tenner Challenge represents a safe environment for young people to experience running their own enterprise. It provides a unique opportunity for them to engage in enterprise education – offering the platform to develop key employability skills. The programme also contributes to the school's statutory obligation to prepare pupils for the opportunities, responsibilities and experiences of later life and supports. Tenner also supports PSHE education in England and Personal and Social Education Framework in Wales by providing an opportunity to develop employability, team working and leadership skills and learn about the economic and business environment.

⇨ Learning outcomes show a positive link between the Tenner Challenge activities and all employability skills tested – with statistically significant progression in problem solving, resilience, communication, creativity and confidence. Arguably skill areas that require repetitive application to develop and improve skill areas which the month-long activity provides a suitable time frame for.

⇨ 83% of young people felt that Tenner has provided them with an unique opportunity to learn and achieve new things.

⇨ Entrepreneurial activities such as Tenner gives students the opportunity to explore self-employment as a potential career option, thereby helping young people to further define their career orientations.

⇨ Anecdotal evidence indicates that one of the consequences in providing entrepreneurial experiences is the power it has in naturally discriminating those who are more inclined to become entrepreneurs. Indeed, by engaging in 'trying the opportunity out', many will get a first-hand experience of the obstacles occurring when running a business and will thereby get an early indication of the viability and future success of their business ideas.

⇨ The Tenner Challenge encompasses the notion of social responsibility and offers young people the opportunity to engage with local communities and people they would not otherwise engage with. 65% of young people agreed when asked if they felt Tenner helped in making their school and local community a nice place, with another 66% engaging on extra-curricular activities as a result of Tenner.

⇨ The Tenner Challenge promotes the welfare of others and provides young people with philanthropic opportunities. In total, over £29,147 was donated to good causes, with national charities and local charitable projects as the main benefactors. This provides an opportunity to consider values as an important consideration when making decisions.

2015

⇨ The above information is reprinted with kind permission from Young Enterprise. Please visit www.tenner.org.uk and www.young-enterprise.org.uk for further information.

© Young Enterprise 2016

Time to roll out real-world business studies?

***An article from* The Conversation.**

By Mike Haynes, Professor of International Political Economy, University of Wolverhampton

Today in Britain there is hardly a major business that has not been accused of wrongdoing. From the banks to GlaxoSmithKline and BP, both of whom have had their coffers lightened somewhat after paying fines, to G4S and Tesco who face investigations for alleged offences, the list goes on and on.

But where does this leave the 100,000-plus students who are studying business? Economics students have protested against an irrelevant economics curriculum, but little has been heard from those studying business even as the enormous scale of bad and/or criminal behaviour by the world's biggest companies stares us in the face.

There is a structural problem here. Business schools could be about business but too often they have to present themselves as for business. They demonstrate the importance of a business agenda in higher education. Students are encouraged to see themselves as entrepreneurs even though the chances of their being involved in genuine business entrepreneurship are small. Courses tell them about leadership when the best that most of us can achieve is some form of followership.

We preach about opportunity but practise hierarchy and social selection. Indeed given the diminishing patterns of social mobility in the UK, and the preference for those with public school and Russell Group backgrounds, the prospects are poor for students in most ordinary university business schools to rise anywhere near the top.

Company of wolves

Business schools seem to treat bad behaviour as the exception rather than the rule. But is it? In the 1930s Edwin Sutherland risked his academic career in the US by keeping a set of index cards about the prosecutions of major companies. With this simple research method he was able to make the explosive argument that business violation of the criminal law was common. More, many major corporations were recidivist, serial offenders.

His work became a sociological classic. But Sutherland made less impact in the world of business studies where men in suits still struggle to ethically negotiate

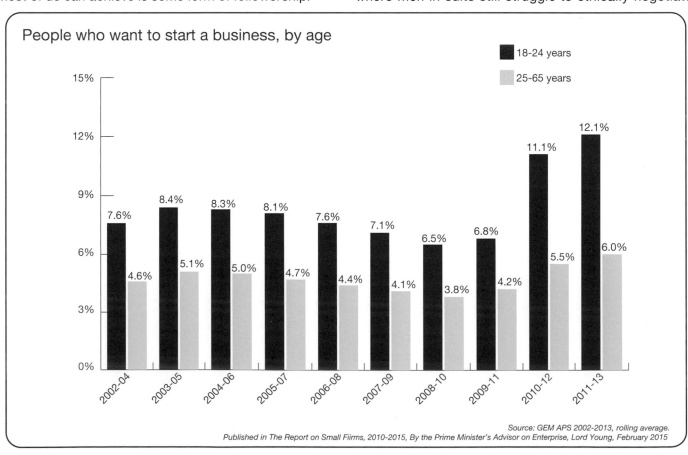

People who want to start a business, by age

■ 18-24 years
■ 25-65 years

	2002-04	2003-05	2004-06	2005-07	2006-08	2007-09	2008-10	2009-11	2010-12	2011-13
18-24 years	7.6%	8.4%	8.3%	8.1%	7.6%	7.1%	6.5%	6.8%	11.1%	12.1%
25-65 years	4.6%	5.1%	5.0%	4.7%	4.4%	4.1%	3.8%	4.2%	5.5%	6.0%

Source: GEM APS 2002-2013, rolling average.
Published in The Report on Small Fiirms, 2010-2015, By the Prime Minister's Advisor on Enterprise, Lord Young, February 2015

the 'triple bottom line' of profit, people and planet, guided by their sense of corporate social responsibility.

But 'crime in the executive suites' has always been bigger than 'crime on the streets'. Events since 2008 have revealed how colossal today's ongoing corporate crime wave is. The investment banks almost brought down the major economies. Then we learned that they had also been fixing the world financial casino. The high street banks have practised endless and systematic mis-selling – fraud by another name. The level of PPI compensation alone suggests that on average each high street branch of a UK bank may have been involved in mis-selling policies worth millions. And we know from Lloyds that this often involved senior staff browbeating low-paid junior employees into doing their organisation's dirty work.

Swathes of private companies are essentially corporate welfare subsidy junkies. UK corporate welfare costs have been estimated by one critic to run to £85 billion a year. Corporate hand-outs extend from cushy PFI deals to direct and indirect subsidies, tax breaks and even a bit of free labour thanks to the UK benefits system.

Company performance, even when masked by creative accountancy and boosted by low pay for the bulk of their workers, is often lamentable. Yet bosses filch ever more, supported by indulgent boards and compensation committees whose real function appears to be sustaining grotesque pay levels. And when activity involves criminality that falls within the scope of UK law and law enforcement, then it is rare that any serious sanction follows. Margaret Hodge has rightly questioned why Serco and G4S are able to bid for more contracts while both being investigated for alleged fraud. And taxes – well to paraphrase Leona Hemlsey – only little people, and little companies, pay taxes.

Student moans

Some good research is done in business schools – ironically driven there by the very irrelevance of much of the work in economics departments. One of the most important centres of critical analysis in the UK, for example, is Manchester Business School's Centre for Research on Socio-Cultural Change. At Essex University, Professor Prem Sikka has played an important role in challenging many accountancy fiddles.

Almost every university has a business school where many times more people study than in economics departments. Yet our courses barely reflect the problems that we have with business. Perhaps to understand this students might better invest in a

subscription to *Private Eye* than another glossy textbook.

What we need is a new Sutherland for 21st-century business schools. It would not be difficult. Think how many index cards we could fill with tax avoidance. Or what about money laundering? London is reckoned to be the world's biggest money laundering centre. And it has been the storm centre for the dodgy dealing behind many a global financial collapse – some say back to the South Sea Bubble. Then what of the cards for the super-rich? The idea that the UK is 'open for business' means any oligarch can use the UK to hide their wealth, buy up assets and deploy the courts and the law to fight their legal battles.

Business schools need to confront this world of business as it is. Our students might be our best allies. Many of them will be in low-paid part-time jobs; they will be living in buy-to-let properties or in private halls owned by multinationals. They will be worrying about debts that extend into the foreseeable future. And social inequality in the jobs market and the nepotistic social hierarchies of UK higher education institutions will loom ever greater as they get closer to graduation. Real-world business studies can also start close to home.

18 December 2014

⇨ The above information is reprinted with kind permission from *The Conversation*. Please visit www.theconversation.com for further information.

"Work till you drop" warning on pensions

Some people may have to work till they are 81 to build up a decent pension pot, according to a report.

With the Government carrying out a review of the state pension age, research from Royal London says an average earner who starts saving for an occupational pension at 22, and makes the minimum statutory contributions, would need to work until 77 if they want the sort of "gold standard" pension enjoyed by their parents.

Royal London defines this "gold standard", which includes the state pension, as two-thirds of pre-retirement income.

For those living in high-income areas, such as Westminster and Wandsworth in London, achieving a pension pot of this size would take till 80 or 81, assuming contributions are not increased.

At the same time, a review for the Labour Party has concluded that employees should double their contributions to workplace schemes, with a target of 15 per cent of earnings going into pension pots.

Traditionally, the state pension age was 65 for men and 60 for women. This is being equalised and in two years' time it is due to rise, reaching 67 by 2028.

This could rise again as a result of a government review, amid warnings that those starting work today could have to wait until their mid-70s before they receive a state pension.

Royal London's research shows that how much people need to save in occupational schemes, if they want a "gold standard" pension, varies according to where they live.

Variations

While someone in Westminster who makes minimum monthly contributions would have to wait till they are 81, a worker in Boston, Lincolnshire, where incomes are lower, would build up a big enough pot by 73.

Ages for Scotland, Wales and Northern Ireland are 77, 76 and 76, respectively.

Former pensions minister Steve Webb, who is director of policy at Royal London, said: "It is great news that millions more workers are being enrolled into workplace pensions, but the amounts going in are simply not enough to give people the kind of retirement they would want for themselves, and certainly not the sort of pensions that many of those retiring now are enjoying.

"Even in lower wage areas, people face working into their early 70s to get a comfortable retirement. In higher wage areas, the state pension makes a much smaller contribution, so workers in those areas face working well into their 70s."

Mr Webb said the answer was to start saving early and increase pension contributions.

2 March 2016

⇨ The above information is reprinted with kind permission from *Channel 4 News*. Please visit www.channel4.com for further information.

Personal pensions (including stakeholder pensions): scheme members' annual contributions

Numbers of members and value of contributions by type of scheme as reported to HMRC by providers for the year.

Numbers: thousands   Contributions: £ millions

6 April 2014 – 5 April 2015	Contributions				
Employer sponsored schemes	Number of members	Minimum contributions	Individuals contributions[1]	Employer contributions	Total
Contracted out members[2]	140	0	100	280	380
Non-contracted out members	7,000	-	2,450	7,450	9,900
Non-employer sponsored schemes					
Contracted out members[2]					
with only minimum contributions	490	0	-	-	0
with minimum and other contributions	580	0	290	50	340
Non-contracted out members	3,740	-	6,180	3,220	9,400
Total	**11,950**	**0**	**9,030**	**11,000**	**20,030**

Footnotes

1. Figures include basic rate tax relief repaid to scheme administrators by HM Revenue & Customs
2. Number of members for contracted-out plans may include members with zero earnings who will not receive minimum
3. Components may not sum to their total due to rounding.

"-" denotes nil or negligible or not applicable.

Source: Personal Pension Statistics, February 2016, HM Revenue & Customs

Crowded out: how crowdsourcing for start-ups turned into business as usual

An article from The Conversation.

By Ross Brown, Lecturer in Entrepreneurship and Small Business, University of St Andrews and Suzanne Mawson, Lecturer in Entrepreneurship, University of Stirling

THE CONVERSATION

Crowdfunding has been hailed by some as the "democratisation of finance". To many, it is viewed as a key alternative source of finance where we can all get involved in backing new companies through either donations or the purchase of equity. Unfortunately, it hasn't quite worked out like that.

There are several new financing models that use the umbrella term of crowdfunding, but they can be fundamentally different. In theory, 'equity' crowdfunding lets large numbers of small investors invest in firms via online platforms – or 'mini stock markets' for start-ups – regardless of their location. From a business perspective, firms should be able to draw upon a wide range of funders in the crowd, who they might never have known existed, to fund, develop and grow their businesses.

What we've found is that equity crowdfunding isn't as 'new' or 'inclusive' as people first envisaged.

Crowdfunding laboratory

The UK was one of the first countries to grant regulatory approval to equity crowdfunding and, through various tax incentives, has become something of a unique 'laboratory' for this form of entrepreneurial finance. We have witnessed a massive growth in equity crowdfunding. It appears to be doubling in size every year, spawning well-known platforms like Crowdcube, Seedrs and The Syndicate Room. In the space of three years Crowdcube alone has raised over £100 million in capital for over 300 start-ups.

During 2015, we undertook the largest in-depth study to date, examining equity crowdfunding in the UK, interviewing over 60 British start-ups to get their views of why firms use equity crowdfunding, how the process works and the benefits it brings to firms.

Some of our findings confirmed what is already known – that it is filling the funding gap for young start-ups who no longer consider banks as a source of early-stage growth capital. Indeed, many start-ups are attracted to the speed with which they can raise funding and like the lack of strings attached. There are also important intangible benefits to firms from the process, such as firm valuation, product validation and media exposure.

Professional game

However, some other findings were unexpected. Contrary to the idea that crowdfunding is a transaction between firms and the 'crowd', seamlessly brought together through the Internet, we found that deals were often driven by pre-existing networks of investors. Roughly around two-thirds of the crowdfunding campaigns in our study were 'pre-seeded' and backed by business angels (professional investors), with the crowd playing a 'supporting role' where small investors are issued B-class shares that have no voting rights attached.

These professional investors are investing heavily in businesses that they know of and which are often

Some investors are
more equal than others

located nearby to them; the crowd then 'herd' towards firms who obtain pre-seed funding. So in many cases, equity crowdfunding isn't really a new or 'alternative' source of funding, but rather a repackaging of more traditional start-up funding.

As an Internet-mediated form of funding, in theory, firms should be able to access equity crowdfunding irrespective of their geographical location. In reality, however, there seems to be a large 'north-south' divide in terms of successful deals, with around half of all the deal flow emanating from London and the South East.

There are a number of potential reasons for this. For example, the majority of platforms are located in London and we have found that word-of-mouth referrals through business networks are still very important in both identifying and accessing crowdfunding platforms. Many businesses also want to speak to platforms 'in person' before committing to a campaign (rather than engaging virtually), and so being within visiting distance of a platform is important. So despite the Internet-mediated nature of crowdfunding, where distance should be irrelevant, it is strongly

concentrated in the London and the South East ecosystem. We are currently exploring this trend further.

Tip of the iceberg

Few non-professional investors have the knowledge to undertake their own due diligence on firms before they invest nor do they offer firms any additional value (for example through advice or support) on top of their financial contribution. Indeed, some start-ups have referred to the crowd as "dumb money". Observers have also questioned the highly inflated valuations of some of the firms funded through equity crowdfunding, many of which are Internet-based firms linked to the so-called 'sharing economy', and operating in consumer-oriented markets with no intellectual property or recoverable assets.

Given the high failure rate of new start-ups generally, and

the nature of most crowdfunded businesses, few non-professional investors are likely to see a return on their investment any time soon.

Despite these reservations, given the current growth trajectory of equity crowdfunding, what we've seen so far may just be the tip of the iceberg. However, icebergs can sink ships. While providing an important source of start-up funding, equity crowdfunding raises a number of thorny issues in terms of investor returns, investor protection, sustainability and the need for proper regulatory safeguards.

Crowdfunding has been heavily promoted by organisations such as Nesta, but the way it actually works is strangely familiar. We thus advocate a more critically informed discussion about equity crowdfunding, especially given the UK's heavily deregulated and proactive fiscal policy environment for this emerging source of entrepreneurial finance.

16 December 2015

⇨ The above information is reprinted with kind permission from *The Conversation*. Please visit www.theconversation.com for further information.

© 2010–2016, The Conversation Trust (UK)

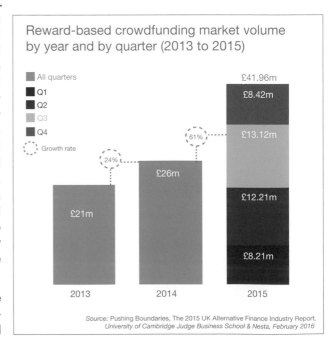

Reward-based crowdfunding market volume by year and by quarter (2013 to 2015)

- All quarters
- Q1
- Q2
- Q3
- Q4
- Growth rate

£21m

24%

£26m

61%

£41.96m

£8.42m
£13.12m
£12.21m
£8.21m

2013   2014   2015

Source: Pushing Boundaries, The 2015 UK Alternative Finance Industry Report, University of Cambridge Judge Business School & Nesta, February 2016

Top 20: Britain's oldest family businesses

The oldest 20 family firms in the UK have collectively traded for 7,013 years, and traded on average for 350 years each, according to new data compiled by the UK's Family Business United.

Whitechapel Bell Foundry in London is the oldest family firm in the country, dating back to 1420, having been owned by two families since it was founded all those years ago. Nevertheless, the firm remains family owned today and is celebrating 595 years as a family business this year.

Furthermore, RJ Balson and Son Ltd, the butchers in Bridport which is currently owned and run by the 26th generation of the founding family, is celebrating 500 years as a family business, dating back to 1515 when Henry VIII was the King of England.

Richard Balson, the current butcher behind the block, is very proud of his heritage, saying: "Too many family businesses fail to successfully pass from generation to generation so we have been fortunate to do so. Although we are the oldest direct lineage family business in the UK, it is more important to strive to be the best at what you do, and for us at Balsons it is all about the product and the service that we offer to our customers, many of whom represent families that have also been customers for generations too."

"It is all about the here and now and planning to succeed. We obviously have a long history but every generation needs to build on what has been handed down to them and, more importantly, be prepared for long hours and plenty of hard work which will result in the opportunity to reap the rewards of being your own boss and in control of your own destiny," adds Richard.

This year also sees Scotland's oldest family firm celebrate a major milestone, marking 300 years since blacksmith John White began the manufacture of a beam end scale. The eighth generation is now running the business, which continues to evolve over time, with Edwin White and wife Tio at the helm.

As Edwin explains, "We will carry on at the front of technology, developing products and looking for new markets, and over time we have had to balance tradition with innovation and embrace new technologies."

Edwin added, "It's hard to believe that a firm can go on for 300 years. It has played a very big part in community life but we are delighted to have stood the test of time, evolved into the business that we are today and proud to be celebrating our tercentenary in 2015."

Founded by Paul Andrews back in 2011, *Family Business United* is the UK's leading online magazine and resource centre for the family business sector and continues to champion the cause for the sector, helping to dispel some of the myths surrounding the sector.

Clearly, the firms in the top 20 dispel the myth that family firms cannot span the generations, their heritage is part of the fabric of the firm but they are continually evolving to meet the needs of doing business in the 21st century, include major employers, generate significant revenues and make significant contributions to their local communities too.

As Andrews adds, "2015 is a celebration for the family business sector as a whole with the oldest family firms in England and Scotland alone sharing 800 years of family business history. These firms are the oldest but there are plenty more great British family firms celebrating their own milestones this year too."

"Family firms are the very fabric of what makes Britain 'great' and each and every one makes a notable contribution, be it through generation to GDP, employment, tax contributions or philanthropic endeavours and we are delighted to celebrate their achievements and to continue to promote the success of the sector."

The 20 oldest family businesses in Britain

1. Whitechapel Bell Foundry (1420 – London) Manufacturing bells
2. RJ Balson and Son Ltd (1515 – Bridport, Dorset) Butchers
3. John Brooke & Sons Holdings Ltd (1541 – Yorkshire) Property
4. R. Durtnell & Sons Limited (1591 – Kent) Builders
5. C. Hoare & Co. (1672 – London) Bank
6. Morning Foods (1675 – Crewe, Cheshire) Miller
7. James Lock & Co Ltd (1676 – London) Milliners
8. Toye & Co (1685 – Birmingham) Regalia and Medals
9. C.P.J. Field & Co. Ltd (1690 – Sussex) Funeral Directors
10. Folkes Group Plc (1697 – Stourbridge, West Midlands) Property
11. Shepherd Neame Limited (1698 – Faversham, Kent) Brewery
12. Berry Bros. & Rudd (1698 – London) Wine and Spirit Merchant
13. W. Austin and Sons Limited (1700 – Hertfordshire) Funeral directors
14. Salts Healthcare Limited (1701 – Birmingham) HealthCare Products
15. Fortnum & Mason (1707 – London) Department store
16. Brakspear (1711 – Oxfordshire) Public houses

17. John White & Son Ltd (1715 – Auchtermuchty, Scotland) Weighing machines
18. Aspall Cyder (1728 – Suffolk) Cyder and vinegar producer
19. Floris (1730 – London) Retailer of toiletries & accessories
20. Wilsons & Co (Sharrow) Ltd (1737 – Sheffield) Manufacturers of snuff

As Andrews concludes, "These family firms have stood the test of time, are steeped in history and tradition, have experienced the highs and the lows of British history, coronations, world wars, recessions and more besides, and stand for the best of British family values, entrepreneurship and have made their mark too. It is recognised that one in three jobs in the UK is within a family firm so 2015 is a time to celebrate the success of those family firms that have truly stood the test of time."

Family Business United maintains an ongoing list of the oldest family firms in the UK, broken down by county.

21 August 2015

⇨ The above information is reprinted with kind permission from Family Business United. Please visit www.familybusinessunited.com for further information.

Why family business is big business

There is a huge misconception around the term "family business". The words seems inextricably linked to the idea of small business; of Mum and Dad toiling round the clock in a corner shop or the reluctant son pressed into service as an apprentice butcher.

By Steve Benger, Managing Partner, Accelerus

Yes, there are millions of SMEs run by families, but the reality is that family-run businesses are amongst the biggest and most successful in the world.

A recent report by Center for Family Business at the University of St.Gallen, Switzerland, reveals the true scale of family business across the globe.

"A recent report by Center for Family Business at the University of St.Gallen, Switzerland, reveals the true scale of family business across the globe"

The 500 top firms in their *Global Family Business Index* employ nearly 21 million people and produce a combined annual sales of $6.5 trillion, enough to be the third-largest economy in the world. Firms like Walmart, VW, BMW, Ikea and Aldi are all family businesses with the majority of shares being held by members of the family, or in the case of Ikea 100 per cent.

Barclays Bank says Britain now has more than two million family-owned businesses and that first-generation companies are growing sales at a rate of 22 per cent a year. The bank reckons family-owned businesses generated revenues of £540 billion last year and that this figure is set to hit £661 billion by 2018.

Leading that growth are companies like The Pentland Group which is owned by Stephen Ruben and his family. Founded in 1932 as The Liverpool Shoe Company with little more than £100 base capital, the organisation has evolved, over eight decades, into a global family of sports, outdoor and fashion brands like Berghaus, Speedo and JD Sports generating global sales of over $3 billion.

What is clear from all the evidence is that the family business model is generating huge value for its shareholders and should never be dismissed solely as a way of organising small-scale economic activity?

So what is it about the family model that produces such sustainable businesses?

Loyalty

The fundamental principle that runs through every family business is the concept of loyalty – the emotional bond that ties together all participants in the business with an unquestioning duty to achieve the best for each other.

"Barclays Bank says Britain now has more than two million family-owned businesses and that first-generation companies are growing sales at a rate of 22 per cent a year"

It is a powerful force which most manager-run businesses would dearly love to replicate but are unable to achieve with purely financial incentives. Loyalty is not just a soft management concept – it does have a tangible value and its impact on a business can be easily measured. In recruitment costs alone, family businesses often have an advantage over their managed business counterparts because they tend to keep their staff longer, not least because junior members are likely to take more senior positions in the future. Many of them become trusted confidants and this plays to the heart of the loyalty factor.

Long termism

Family business have a luxury that many firms dream of – the ability to plan for the long term. Knowing that shareholder pressures for a quick return are simply not there, family businesses can better align the deployment of resources with their strategic objectives. This long-term approach to investing is often referred to as 'patient capital' and it can have huge pay-offs as many of the businesses in the top 500 Index can testify. Around 44 per cent of businesses in the index are run by fourth generation family members and the average age of the top companies is 88 years. The most successful family businesses move beyond the 'dangerous' third generation trueism that they often fail, and build sustainable management and governance processes which are way beyond the often held view that nepotism prevails and damages the business.

Knowledge and expertise

True expertise is endemic in a family business because knowledge gets handed down and from generation to generation, not just in training session or product manuals. The greatest violin maker of all time – better, many would argue than Stradivari whom he trained, was Nicolas Amati, who learnt his craft from his father, who'd been tutored by his father. The same is true of today's family firms, where in-depth product and sector knowledge is part of growing up in a family business. The most successful family businesses complement this knowledge and expertise with

sound and solid business and financial management and training to ensure that they can last the test of time and the very many changes in cyclical businesses and economies.

Challenges

Running a family business is, however, not without its challenges. With every positive that comes from the emotional bond of the family there is a negative.

Accelerus is often called in to family concerns where the sudden death of founder and no obvious successor has left the business floundering. The informal and instinctive processes used to run the business simply disappear as they are rarely documented.

There is often a dangerous assumption that a younger relative will take up the reigns, so succession planning is not deemed necessary. The baton is simply passed on at death or retirement. But the massive swing from manufacturing society to a knowledge-based economy does present challenges for family business as many of the natural candidates for leadership simply don't want to follow in the parents'

footsteps, or are often not the most able to do so.

In the case where there is no clear succession, we have to bring in a leader from outside who has to quickly become part of the family and learn the unwritten rules of the business whilst building the sustainable systems, processes and skills which are critical to future success and sustainability. Anyone of you who has had experience of a new step-parent in the family will appreciate the challenges this brings!

When you get it right – like Walmart who combine family members with the best outside talent – the results can be spectacular. The retailer has 15 board members but only two are now Waltons – a fact that has not stopped the family amassing a fortune estimated to be a cool $147 billion.

26 October 2015

⇨ The above information is reprinted with kind permission from *Business Matters*. Please visit www.bmmagazine.co.uk for further information.

© *Business Matters 2016*

Understanding motivations for entrepreneurship

This research improves our understanding of motivations for starting a business in the UK, helping to fill an important evidence gap.

The recession and subsequent downturn saw an increase in numbers of very small businesses and a rise in the rate of entrepreneurial activity. Despite little change in balance of opportunity-driven and necessity-driven entrepreneurship there was a renewed focus on questions about whether necessity-driven businesses will tend to survive and succeed. It is often assumed that necessity-driven businesses will be less successful than those started to purse an opportunity and this report establishes evidence to address this.

The data

This study used a re-survey of 1,000 respondents to Global Entrepreneurship Monitor (GEM) surveys to provide reliable evidence on the different motivations for starting a business and to explore how these differences might be related to business performance. This survey was carefully developed based on a rapid evidence assessment summarising the current knowledge on motivations for entrepreneurship and ten exploratory interviews. The survey findings were further supplemented by in-depth interviews with 40 entrepreneurs.

Key points

⇨ This study shows that motivations for starting a business are complex and that motivations other than the traditional opportunity-driven and necessity-driven distinction are more closely related to business survival and success. These motivations can be best classified in terms of the importance attached to 'autonomy and better work', 'challenge', 'financial' and 'family and legacy'

aspects. Across all business types, entrepreneurs say autonomy is their most important motivator.

⇨ Businesses can do well regardless of whether they were started out of opportunity or necessity. Both opportunity-driven businesses and necessity-driven businesses create jobs, innovate and export.

⇨ The most important factor for business success was ambition with those firms starting out with high growth expectations performing most strongly. Indeed, motivations influence business success mainly by driving differences in growth expectations, which in turn drive success.

⇨ Businesses created by autonomy- and family-motivated entrepreneurs have a higher chance of survival.

⇨ Motivations are generally stable through the course of running a business, with a small increase in the importance attributed to 'autonomy and flexibility'. This finding is promising as it suggests that many entrepreneurs' expectations around autonomy, flexibility and quality of work are being met in their roles as business owner-managers.

⇨ The recession increased entrepreneurs' 'challenge', 'financial' and 'family and legacy' motivations to start a business, while 'autonomy and flexibility', opportunity

and necessity motivations did not change. Many recession-era entrepreneurs saw their redundancy as an opportunity and had a high level of ambition when starting their business.

⇨ Taken together, the research shows that regardless of whether originally driven by opportunity or necessity, a business can be successful. Most important is the expectation to grow and so emphasis should be placed on encouraging and supporting that. The expectation to grow is in turn more strongly related to 'challenge', 'financial' and 'family and legacy' motivations than to the opportunity-necessity dichotomy.

March 2015

⇨ The above information is reprinted with kind permission from the Department for Business Innovation & Skills. Please visit www.gov.uk for further information.

Supporting ethnic minority and female entrepreneurs

Ethnic minority businesses are estimated to contribute £25–£32 billion to the UK economy per year, and women-led enterprises contribute around £70 billion. However, ethnic minorities and women are seen to be under-represented as entrepreneurs, and to have lower levels of business performance.

While policymakers usually regard these two groups separately, policy initiatives have often occurred in tandem. The similarity in core concerns and business outcomes suggests potential benefits from exploring the connections between ethnic minority and women-led (EMW) businesses.

Potential business barriers include actual or perceived discrimination, the quantity and quality of businesses, market failure in business support and the uniqueness of EMW enterprises. Recent efforts towards boosting this sector have only returned modest changes, suggesting that policy in this area remains underdeveloped and problematic.

The paper *Barriers to Ethnic Minority and Women's Enterprise*, published by the Enterprise Research Centre, reviews the research evidence on enterprise diversity. The research review focuses on key issues including access to finance, market selection and management skills.

Key findings

⇨ Particular ethnic groups find it more difficult to obtain credit for their businesses. Rather than direct discrimination, this is largely due to a greater prevalence of risk factors such as business age and financial track records.

⇨ A perception of ethnic discrimination discourages some ethnic minority businesses from applying for bank loans.

⇨ Under-resourced immigrant entrepreneurs tend to focus on the same low-cost business niches such as small-scale retailing and catering, risking market saturation.

⇨ Female entrepreneurs perceive higher financial barriers for their business. There is almost no evidence of supply-side discrimination, but there are indications of pronounced debt aversion among women.

⇨ Women-led firms are typically smaller and overrepresented within service sectors.

⇨ Although business performance by gender does not differ, women-owned enterprises typically start with lower levels of resources.

⇨ The actual prevalence of female entrepreneurs can be masked by dual ownership: joint male/female partnerships account for about 20 per cent of all small and medium-sized enterprises.

Policy relevance and implications

⇨ Narrow-focused policy support for self-employment should be avoided. High levels of low-quality entrepreneurship amongst EMWs does not automatically indicate upward social mobility, and encouraging further entry into already crowded low-quality sectors may be counterproductive.

⇨ UK enterprise policy should consider following the US 'quality versus quantity' model of encouraging minority entrepreneurs with good credentials in high value-added sectors.

⇨ Policies aimed specifically at encouraging ethnic minority start-ups could lead to an increase in enterprise within ethnic enclaves only – without contributing to a social integration agenda.

⇨ The increasingly differentiated group of 'minority' entrepreneurs makes a simple intervention policy difficult. Local-level targeted enterprise support is likely to be more effective than a national 'one size fits all' policy of intervention.

Further information

The Enterprise Research Centre (ERC) is an independent research centre for research, knowledge and expertise on SME growth and entrepreneurship. It is funded by the ESRC, the Department for Business, Innovation and Skills, Innovate UK and the British Bankers Association.

The views expressed in this evidence briefing are those of the authors and not necessarily those of the ESRC.

February 2015

⇨ The above information is reprinted with kind permission from the Economic and Social Research Council. Please visit www.esrc.ac.uk for further information.

Revealed: how we're rebranding poor people as entrepreneurs

An article from **The Conversation.**

By Laura Galloway, Professor of Business and Enterprise, Heriot-Watt University

THE CONVERSATION

The last several decades have seen a steady increase in the profile and celebration of entrepreneurship in the UK. It is associated with economic development, growth and making a positive contribution to the country. There is plenty of evidence to support this – for example the immensely valuable Global Entrepreneurship Monitor research project, which compares rates and types of entrepreneurship throughout the world. As a consequence, developing and investing in entrepreneurship has never been more prioritised, as evidenced by the UK Government's recent Enterprise Bill, with its raft of measures to support entrepreneurs.

Yet there is another side to this growing army of entrepreneurs. Far from the Levi Roots and Michelle Mones of the world, many others appear to fall into the category because it is the only one available to them. They are not planning how to invest their next million or hiring teams of new employees to deliver their vision. They are living in poverty and desperation, with little prospect for the future. Worse, policymakers and enterprise specialists seem barely to have noticed.

What do we mean by entrepreneurship anyway? Governments and the media use it most often to describe those who are employed independently – whether sole traders or people who employ others. The term 'entrepreneur' evokes ideas of innovation and opportunity, which are then transferred to these people. Unfortunately the reality is not quite so affirmative.

Behind the statistics

According to latest statistics, the business creation rate has risen by 55% since 2000. Yet the proportion of enterprises that have employees has actually fallen from a third to a quarter, while the proportion of those with no employees has risen. This means that a lot of the entrepreneurship 'success' that we hear about is actually represented by a 73% rise in the number of people who have become self-employed.

Now, being self-employed has many advantages – most compellingly, individuals create their own job. There is a net economic benefit to that, and potentially social benefits too, like flexibility. Yet within this, there is a group that has been largely neglected: those for whom self-employment is in fact negative, undermines their quality of life, and is even exploitative.

For at least the last decade, there has been speculation in the employment literature that organisations are increasingly changing their employment model from employee-based to relying on self-employed contractors. We see it in the IT sector and in new media, for example. It means that many people previously in employment are now self-employed, meaning they do broadly the same job but without employment rights, unions, and in some cases at lower pay. This has been happening in some sectors for decades (construction, for example), yet academics have not really explored the phenomenon.

In a similar vein, the New Enterprise Allowance – a UK welfare benefit that provides income to support 'business' creation – has been introduced to incentivise long-term unemployed people into self-employment. Again, the extent to which this has had the desired positive effect has not been explored.

Reality bites

I have been involved in a study of self-employment in relation to contractors and those needing an alternative to unemployment. We interviewed key people in Scotland working in business support, poverty alleviation and social support. We also collected the stories of a small sample of people who are self-employed and in these unexplored categories.

We found there is clearly a group of 'entrepreneurs' who are living in poverty (as defined by UK government measures). We have no idea how representative our group is among the self-employed, but our research suggested it may be prevalent and further investigation is certainly required.

Turning workforces into contractors is an issue, as we expected, but self-employment as an alternative to unemployment was even more concerning. In many cases, people were counted as self-employed after their welfare benefits had been removed or where "regular" employment was inappropriate or unavailable. These individuals were essentially forced into self-employment.

9 March 2016

⇨ The above information is reprinted with kind permission from *The Conversation*. Please visit www.theconversation.com for further information.

Corporate scandals and how (not) to handle them

After a disastrous week for VW, we look back at 30 years of business disasters and their cost in lives, money and reputations.

By David Hellier

Bhopal

Estimates suggest up to 25,000 people died and more than 550,000 people were injured, some seriously and permanently, after a gas leak incident at the Union Carbide pesticide plant in Bhopal, India, in 1984.

Dow Chemical bought Union Carbide in 2001 and maintains that it now has no responsibility for the Bhopal victims, following a $470 million settlement paid by Union Carbide in 1989. Campaigning groups protested against Dow Chemical's sponsorship of the 2012 London Olympics because of the Bhopal issue.

Rana Plaza factory

A factory building outside Dhaka, Bangladesh, collapsed in 2013, killing more than 1,000 workers in the deadliest disaster in the history of the garment industry.

A government report found widespread fault for the disaster, blaming the local mayor, the building's owner and the bosses of the five garment manufacturers using the building. The ILO and campaign groups raised $30 million from retailers including Primark, Bonmarché and Benetton, all of which sourced garments from the factories in the building, to help injured workers and the families of those who died.

Libor and other bank scandals

Big banks have paid out a total of $260 billion in fines, compensation and lawsuits since the 2007–8 financial crisis, according to recent research from US investment bank Morgan Stanley.

Former Barclays boss Bob Diamond was one of the first executive heads to roll, after the bank agreed in 2012 to pay a £290 million fine for trying to manipulate Libor, the rate at which banks lend to each other. Former UBS and Citigroup trader Tom Hayes was recently sentenced to 14 years for conspiring to manipulate interest rates.

Enron and Arthur Andersen

The world's most infamous accounting scandal was the bankruptcy of Enron in 2001, subsequently the subject of screen and stage portrayals. The energy trader's unfathomable accounts had obscured huge debts stashed off its balance sheet. Once these were revealed, the company imploded. The pensions and jobs of thousands of employees, and $74 billion of shareholder funds were wiped out. Enron's auditor, Arthur Andersen, also collapsed. In his book *Connect*, former BP boss Lord Browne says the fate of Enron, which set great store by its corporate social responsibility programme,

"demonstrates in dramatic fashion just how irrelevant CSR (corporate social responsibility) really is".

Exxon Valdez

In 1989 the *Exxon Valdez* oil tanker ran aground off the coast of Alaska, releasing up to 750,000 barrels of crude oil into the sea. Five years later, a federal judge in Alaska ordered Exxon to pay $4.5 billion in damages for the spill – this was at the time the largest such penalty in US history. Around 250,000 birds and other animals died as a result of the spill.

BP Texas City and Deepwater Horizon

BP has suffered two massive disasters in a relatively short time. In 2005, 15 workers were killed and more than 170 others were injured in an explosion at its refinery in Texas City. In his book, Lord Browne names Texas City as one of two significant incidents – the other was an oil spill in Alaska – that marred the end of his tenure as chief executive.

The Deepwater Horizon oil spill, which has cost the group around $54 billion in penalties, damages and clean-up costs, began on 20 April, 2010, and continued to flow for 87 days. Deepwater is considered the largest accidental marine oil spill in the history of the oil industry.

Johnson & Johnson and Tylenol

In 1982 seven people in Chicago died after taking extra-strong Tylenol (paracetamol) capsules which had been laced with cyanide as part of an extortion plot. The pharmaceuticals group acted swiftly and behaved openly, recalling all of the product – at a cost of $100 million – and setting up toll-free numbers for concerned customers. Lord Browne argues that because the company responded so quickly and transparently, it soon regained market share – and its reputation.

The Toyota accelerator scandal

Toyota, the Japanese car giant, agreed to pay out around $1.1 billion in late 2012 to settle a class action lawsuit stemming from complaints of unintended acceleration in its vehicles. The case badly soured its reputation for safety and affected sales. Owners of around 16 million Toyota vehicles were eligible for compensation and safety checks. It was alleged that 21 deaths had been caused by the defect, also known as 'sticky pedal'.

26 September 2015

⇨ The above information is reprinted with kind permission from *The Guardian*. Please visit www.theguardian.com for further information.

As companies embrace the circular economy, are they missing a trick?

By Rachel Butler

Our approach to using natural resources has changed dramatically over the last ten years, with companies becoming more aware of the need to shift from a linear production model of take–make–dispose, to a more responsible model which considers the full product lifecycle. This has placed greater focus on reducing waste and negative environmental impact. In response, many businesses are creating innovative ways of re-using and recycling the surplus and waste materials companies and consumers produce.

But are many of today's companies missing an obvious and simple opportunity to contribute positively to a circular society? Talk of a circular economy is high on the agenda thanks to organisations like the Ellen MacArthur Foundation. However, making this a reality may be many years away. In the meantime, our manufacturing and retail industries have a massive opportunity to use their products to support communities both locally and across the globe, demonstrating they are socially responsible brands.

For the last 19 years, the charity In Kind Direct has been working with over 1,000 companies to unlock the potential of their surplus goods, re-distributing them to UK charities and social enterprises working at home and abroad to help develop thriving, resilient communities. The model is a simple one: companies donate their products to In Kind Direct which acts as a logistics 'middle man', enabling thousands of small grass roots organisations to access the goods they need to run their services or give to people in need. The effect is dramatic. To date an estimated 13,000 tonnes of product have been diverted into productive use, enabling over 7,500 charities to save money and help millions of people every year, including some of the most vulnerable in our society.

So why is product donation not a core part of every manufacturer's model?

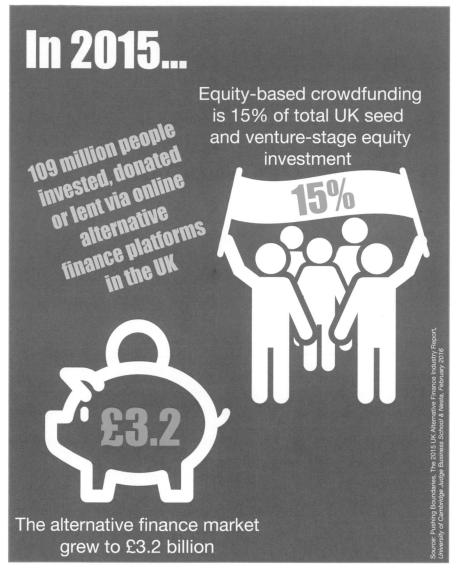

In 2015...

109 million people invested, donated or lent via online alternative finance platforms in the UK

Equity-based crowdfunding is 15% of total UK seed and venture-stage equity investment

15%

£3.2

The alternative finance market grew to £3.2 billion

Source: Pushing Boundaries, The 2015 UK Alternative Finance Industry Report, University of Cambridge Judge Business School & Nesta, February 2016

Successful manufacturers have built their reputations on delivering a consistent supply of faultless products to consumers. This has required sophisticated demand-forecasting models, efficient production lines and stringent quality assurance protocols. But no business is perfect, and as demand and supply fluctuate, errors occur, strategies change and 'unwanted' products still emerge. More often than not those products are in perfectly usable condition but don't pass the brand test. Sometimes the packaging is not quite right, there is a slight imperfection in the product or the 'best before' date is approaching. Manufacturers are left with a dilemma between selling on to wholesalers for pennies in the pound, re-processing, or worse, sending usable goods to landfill. All options come at a cost and because the products are seen as 'unwanted',

the priority is all too often to minimise loss rather than create any value. More businesses could reverse this approach and begin thinking of surplus product as an opportunity for delivering social impact.

Last year alone, over £11 million worth of goods were distributed by In Kind Direct. This included everything from clothing and toys for women and children fleeing violence, toiletries for homeless young men, or essential cleaning supplies for families struggling to make ends meet, to IT equipment helping elderly people become more digitally savvy.

The effect doesn't end there either. Businesses are starting to realise the positive effect socially responsible activities can have, not only on the organisations and beneficiaries they directly support, but also on their own workforce, their customers and even their shareholders. Employees

who are proud of their company's charitable initiatives are likely to be happier and more productive in their jobs. With the rise of social media, customers are increasingly expecting a one-to-one relationship with businesses and giving preference to companies which operate in a responsible way. More and more investment is going into sustainable practices in order to face the huge challenges of climate change, resource scarcity, overpopulation and inequality. Sustainability is not just about ensuring the environment is preserved and your workforce is well treated. It's about taking a global view of the ecosystem in which businesses operate and understanding the virtuous circle started by doing what is right.

By giving a new lease of life to products that would otherwise have been sold off at a fraction of the price, remanufactured or sent to landfill, companies can instead create social value. As products are used by charities and their beneficiaries, these donations make a tremendous impact on local communities, and in turn, on consumers and employees, giving the circular economy a brand new spin.

Though every company should aim for zero waste, there is still a long way to go before surplus and slight seconds completely disappear. While companies grapple with how to develop a circular approach, product giving is something to start doing today. It's efficient, simple and it changes lives.

16 October 2015

⇨ The above information is reprinted with kind permission from 2degrees. Please visit www.2degreesnetwork.com for further information.

© 2degrees 2016

Is Chinese investment into the UK at record levels?

By Joseph O'Leary

"There has been more inward investment from Chinese companies in the last 18 months, than in the last 30 years combined."

Reported on BBC Today *Programme and from a government press release in January.*

This morning the Chinese Premier, Li Keqiang, wrote a *Times* piece on China's economic development and the significance of its trading relationship with the UK. It hasn't been all praise for the UK lately however; at the weekend the Chinese ambassador reportedly remarked that Britain now lags behind its German and French neighbours.

Amidst the conflicting perspectives, a familiar claim emerged from the BBC's morning coverage. UK Trade and Investment, which made the claim put out by the Government earlier this year, didn't provide Full Fact with the details of where it was from, but offered itself as the source we could attribute the claim to.

We haven't been able to trace reliable figures to support the claim. Those that do exist indicate the UK is a significant target for Chinese companies compared to other countries, and that recent years have seen several large examples of Chinese investment. But on only one indicator – investment which involves significant equity gains – are there obvious numbers to support the claim.

The Foreign and Commonwealth Office (FCO) separately commented that there was "virtually zero" investment prior to a few years ago, and so gave the view the claim is plausible.

£1.7 billion of Chinese investment to the UK in 2012 – but the figures are unreliable

This is the FCO's interpretation of figures it was given by the Chinese Ministry of Commerce, statistics it describes as "not perfect". So we found in other ways: the figures were not obviously available on the Ministry's website, let alone details of how they were calculated. What's more, while it comments that these are significant rises since 2010, we're given little idea of the picture before then.

Nevertheless, on these numbers the UK is placed as high as fourth in the world for receipts of Chinese investment, behind Hong Kong, the USA and Kazakhstan.

That throws up another problem with the data though: it doesn't necessarily reflect which countries end up with the money. The FCO comments of the money sent to Hong Kong: "nearly all of this money will go on to third markets but it's not clear where".

This happens across the world too. The British Virgin Islands come fifth in the world for receiving foreign direct investment (a particular type of investment which is more than just gaining equity in a foreign company).

But the UN and others admit that countries like this aren't primarily the final destination of investment. They go via financial centres for tax or administrative purposes.

So even with reliable figures from China, this wouldn't necessarily give the full picture either.

Barclays, BP and Weetabix the biggest recent cases

We can get some idea of how this investment might break down through figures put together by the American Enterprise Institute and the Heritage Foundation. They compile a list of actual occasions in which a Chinese investor has sent funds to the UK.

Among the larger examples, the China Development Bank's 2007 purchase of 3% equity in Barclays, the SAFE investment company's 2008 investment into BP and most famously the 2012 takeover by Bright Foods of Weetabix. These combined sum to some £4 billion worth of investment in UK companies.

This list won't necessarily be exhaustive, but it does put some solid examples to the abstract numbers.

Direct investment at historically high levels

Alternative figures put together by the Office for National Statistics give us a picture of foreign direct investment over time. This only counts cases where the investor gains an 'effective voice' in the target: defined as holding 10% equity. That's why its figure for 2012, £193 million of investment in 2012, is so much lower than the others on offer.

There are figures on this measure going back to 2003, and here they do show record levels for the most recent year compared to every previous on record combined.

While this does give some credence to the claim, it still isn't the data we were pointed to. Until we know more about the Chinese figures, in particular having a timeseries for recent years, we can't say how accurate the central claim is, or whether there's more context needed.

16 June 2014

⇨ The above information is reprinted with kind permission from Full Fact. Please visit www.fullfact.org for further information.

Tesco delayed payments to suppliers to boost profits, watchdog finds

Groceries code adjudicator finds supermarket failed to pay back multi-million pound sums owed for up to two years, but regulator is unable to levy fine.

By Sarah Butler

The grocery market watchdog has ordered Tesco to make "significant changes" in the way it deals with suppliers after finding the supermarket had deliberately delayed payments to boost its profits.

Christine Tacon, the groceries code adjudicator (GCA), said Tesco had seriously breached the legally binding code governing the grocery market. She said some suppliers had to wait two years for millions of pounds owed by the grocer.

However, Tacon is unable to fine the supermarket as the breaches took place before her power to levy fines came into force in April last year.

"I was troubled to see Tesco at times prioritising its own finances over treating suppliers fairly," Tacon said.

She added that she had seen internal e-mails suggesting payments should not be made ahead of a certain date in order to avoid missing targets promised to City investors. In some cases this occurred despite suppliers' requests for payment, at other times it was with their consent.

"The pressure on buyers and finance teams to meet margin targets was the overriding pressure within the business. It was widespread. It was everywhere," she said.

Tacon also criticised the company for unilaterally making deductions from invoice payments. Even when Tesco acknowledged a debt, Tacon said that on some occasions the money was not repaid for more than a year, or as long as two years.

The adjudicator launched the investigation in February last year after Tesco admitted it had overstated profits in a scandal that has also led to a Serious Fraud Office investigation.

Dave Lewis, Tesco chief executive, who joined the business in September 2014 just a few days before the accounting scandal emerged and was in post for only four months of the period investigated by Tacon, apologised to suppliers and said the retailer had now "fundamentally changed".

"Over the last year we have worked hard to make Tesco a very different company from the one described in the GCA report. The absolute focus on operating margin [under former boss Phil Clarke] had damaging consequences for the business and our relationship with suppliers," he said.

Tacon said Tesco had "acted unreasonably" by delaying payments to suppliers, often for lengthy periods and sometimes deliberately to support its profits ahead of key financial reporting periods. For example, a list of methods for meeting a half-year profit target seen by Tacon included "not paying back money owed".

She considered Tesco's breach of the code to be serious because of the varied and widespread nature of the delays in payment.

"The most shocking thing I found was how widespread it was. Every supplier I spoke to had evidence of delays in payments," Tacon said.

One supplier was owed several million pounds as a result of price changes being incorrectly applied over a long period, but Tesco took two years to refund the money.

"The sums were often significant and the length of time taken to repay them was too long," she said at the launch of her 60-plus page report.

While in some cases the delays were due to deliberate policy,

Tacon found buyers were given "contradictory and unclear" guidance about the importance of hitting margin targets. Some delays were the result of poor administration and communication and Tesco had "inadequate processes" for correcting errors, for example where data had been input wrongly.

She has given the retailer a month to say how it plans to implement her recommendations, which include paying suppliers in accordance with agreed terms, correcting pricing errors within a week of notification by a supplier and calling a halt to unilateral deductions from invoices. Suppliers will now have 30 days to challenge any proposed deduction.

The adjudicator also said Tesco must improve its invoices, making them clearer and more transparent for suppliers, and train its finance teams and buyers. She said many of the problems encountered related to unclear terms in Tesco's agreements with suppliers and deals not being put into writing – something she has referred to the competition watchdog, the CMA.

Tacon said many suppliers had reported an improvement in relations with Tesco since the period under investigation, June 2013 until February 2015.

She said she had found no evidence that Tesco had required suppliers to make payments to secure better shelf positioning or to increase the amount of space allocated to them on shelves.

However, she will now launch an industry-wide consultation examining payments made by suppliers in order to participate when Tesco reviewed the range of products stocked in a particular category or in order to be made a "category captain", where they could advise on how best to display products. Tesco also asked for "investment" from suppliers to help underpin profits in a particular category. Tacon said such payments could amount to tens or even hundreds of thousands of pounds per supplier.

Tacon said: "There were a range of practices that I am concerned could amount to an indirect requirement for payment [related to positioning of products on shelves], contravening the code."

Lewis said: "In 2014 we undertook our own review into certain historic practices, which were both unsustainable and harmful to our suppliers. We shared these practices with the adjudicator, and publicly apologised. Today, I would like to apologise again. We are sorry."

"We accept the report's findings, which are consistent with our own investigation."

He said Tesco had already implemented all the recommendations of the GCA and had completely changed its practices since January 2015. He said Tesco had also stopped asking for payments related to "category captain" status or range reviews, but the company would look at making further changes in the light of Tacon's planned consultation.

"We have changed the way we work by reorganising, refocusing and retraining our teams and we will continue to work in a way which is consistent with the recommendations," Lewis said.

While Tesco could not be fined, it could have been required to take out newspaper advertisements laying out its apology. Tacon said she had not used this power as Lewis had publicly apologised and Tesco's suppliers gave evidence that dealings had now improved.

The supermarket must now report quarterly to the GCA on the measures she has asked it to introduce and Tacon can launch a new investigation if she finds her recommendations have not been followed through.

Anna Soubry, the business minister, said: "Christine Tacon has done a thorough and fearless investigation into a scandalous situation. Tesco say they have changed their practices and I very much hope they have. Paying smaller suppliers on time and treating them fairly is good and proper business. Late payment can hinder the growth and productivity of these suppliers and can threaten their existence."

26 January 2016

⇨ The above information is reprinted with kind permission from *The Guardian*. Please visit www.theguardian.com for further information.

Supermarkets: is it the end of an empire?

News that the 'Big Four' major British supermarkets are experiencing massive losses has become so ubiquitous in recent months it hardly seems newsworthy anymore. The most spectacular fall from glory has been Tesco's – the retail behemoth that, at the height of its market domination, was present in every postcode in Britain and pocketed one in every seven pounds spent in the country. It recently reported a loss of £6.38 billion, the biggest loss in UK retail history. It is currently under criminal investigation by the Serious Fraud Office for fiddling its accounts while simultaneously being cross-examined by the Groceries Code Adjudicator for bullying its suppliers. Meanwhile, Sainsbury's reported its first loss in nine years to the tune of £72 million, profits at Morrisons were down 52% and Asda recorded its worst performance in 20 years.

While forlorn CEOs scratch their heads and speak in grave tones about their companies' previously unthinkable free fall, communities and independent retailers who have long struggled against the supermarket monopoly are watching on in satisfaction. Traditional markets, small shops, box schemes, farmers' markets and food co-ops are thriving and becoming mainstream alternatives to the supermarkets, having been dismissed for years as hopelessly nostalgic or exclusively for a right-on and privileged minority. And for urban customers of modest means who arrive on foot, stores set up by immigrants increasingly look like plausible, budget alternatives to supermarkets. So much so that in gritty Toxteth in Liverpool the L8 Superstore – a sprawling local emporium renowned for its exciting market-style display of fresh fruit and vegetables outside and its United Nations' of dried goods within – was recently named Food Retailer of the Year in the BBC Food and Farming awards. As owner Abdul Ghafoor puts it, "We have everything here that everyone local needs" from fruit and veg to nappies. Tellingly, last bank holiday weekend local high streets and their small businesses enjoyed a surge in visitors, while footfall at sprawling out-of-town retail parks was down.

Yet it is the German discount supermarkets Aldi and Lidl, not the independent shops, that are credited with dealing the fatal blow to the Big Four and shaking up the food economy. The result is a new breed of shopper – dubbed "promiscuous" by one Sainsbury's exec for being the kind of people who shop around, buy less at one go but on a more frequent basis, and (shock horror!) visit multiple stores on one outing. But the delinquency of these promiscuous shoppers is still modest, relatively speaking; recent research suggests the average consumer frequents just four separate grocers per month. So, while some consumers are revolutionising the food economy by bed hopping between supermarkets and independents, for most people supermarkets remain a regular haunt.

So is the supermarket model here to stay, or will – and can – British shoppers eventually jump ship altogether? The escalating crisis engulfing the Big Four appears to suggest that the previous success of Tesco, Sainsbury's, Morrisons and Asda is not due to the emotional loyalty of its customers, but rather to their resigned pragmatism. Simply put, shoppers considered supermarkets to be convenient and cheap, and that was what kept them coming back. You could do a one-stop mammoth weekly shop in

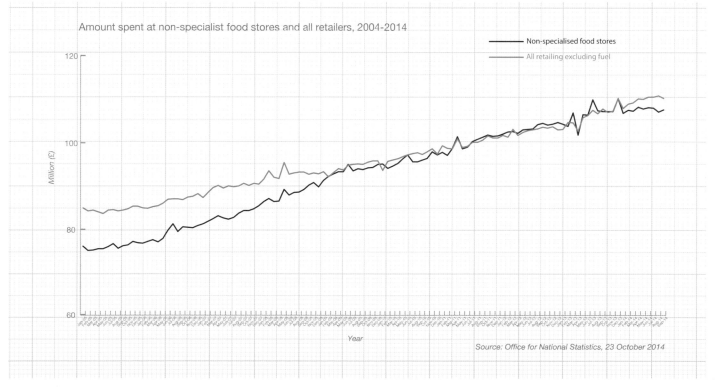

Amount spent at non-specialist food stores and all retailers, 2004-2014

— Non-specialised food stores
— All retailing excluding fuel

Million (£)

Year

Source: Office for National Statistics, 23 October 2014

industrial hangers on out-of-town retail parks; or alternatively stock up in inner-city 'metro' or 'extra' shops through the week, dashing in and out as part of a fast-paced urban lifestyle. Opening hours eclipsed those of independent shops and markets, and the chains' staggering powers of retail acquisition meant they were conveniently located for almost everybody.

Supermarkets may be able to cling on to this notion of convenience, but the myth that they are cheap has been irrevocably shattered. Aldi and Lidl's "everyday low pricing" has shone a torch on the Big Four's hefty mark-ups, and the simplicity of the German discounters' pricing exposed the disingenuous smoke-and-mirrors of the promotions, loyalty schemes and shouty price wars between Tesco, Asda, Morrisons, Sainsbury's and also Waitrose.

With the illusion of value for money shattered, there seems little to redeem supermarkets other than the convenience of having everything under one roof. Listing all the potentially destructive or unethical features of this dominant food retail model would be a lengthy process. But in brief, supermarkets created a food monoculture in which most people buy and eat the same food across Britain. With their global, long-chain sourcing model, they undermined the age-old cycle of seasonal eating. They were the midwives of the 'no-time-to-cook' processed food revolution, which now looks to be a key driver of ill health and obesity. The supermarket business model works on a juggernaut of food miles and has escalated food and packaging wastage to previously unthinkable levels. Supermarkets also denuded urban landscapes, blighted traditional high streets, put independents out of business all over the country and bullied their way into communities while creating food deserts.

Arguably the business model of the Big Four supermarkets, as well as the German discounters, thrives on the exploitation of almost everybody in its remit. In-store staff struggle to subsist on draconian zero-hour contracts and minimum wages, while those in overseas factories making clothes, toys and electronic goods receive disturbingly low pay and often work in conditions that would be unacceptable in Britain. The supermarkets' feudal relationship with their suppliers, and their chokehold on agricultural production is slowly beginning to emerge. One Member of the Scottish Parliament described Tesco's Mafioso-style treatment of its suppliers as akin to "what you see in films like *The Godfather*". The only people who have benefited from the supermarket business model as it stands have been CEOs and shareholders, which explains their current acute distress.

Despite all this, will UK shoppers ever go completely cold turkey on their supermarket shopping habit, even as they wriggle out of the shackles of the Big Four? Or is the expectation of finding most of what one needs under one roof here to stay? Amy and Ruth Anslow, founders of independent Brighton supermarket hiSbe, think it is, and instead of creating an alternative they have reinvented the supermarket model. "It is convenient to be able to buy everything in one place," says Amy, "but what would a better version of that look like, and how would a responsible business behave? We looked at kind of hacking the supermarket model and reinventing it to do something different." hiSbe stands for How It Should Be, and it sells a wide range of fresh food, groceries and household basics every day from 9am to 8pm. Since opening its doors in 2013, it has turned over its first million.

As a social enterprise, hiSbe is a very different kind of supermarket. It offers its customers the full spectrum of food and groceries with products that are as local, seasonal, sustainable, ethically sourced, animal and fish friendly as possible, and with as little packaging, pesticides and additives as feasible. There is zero wastage of edible food and staff are paid above the living wage. Despite these principles, hiSbe is no wholefood store: it sells everyday and familiar products for people on regular diets – it just goes about it in a better way. Nor is it a preachy and pricier alternative for an affluent and principled minority. Prices – which dwarf all other factors as the Big Four found out to their expense – are kept low at hiSbe by selling fruit and vegetables by weight, working directly with family-run farms in Sussex and selling packaged goods below the suppliers' recommended retail prices. With the big supermarkets typically slapping a minimum 30% mark-up on all their goods, customers haven't failed to notice that hiSbe is winning in the all-important price wars, if only in Brighton for the time being.

It seems unlikely that the majority of British shoppers will emerge from three dark decades of the Big Four's monopolisation as though it never happened. However, it is worth remembering that seismic shifts in shopping habits do occur. Ten years ago, even the shrewdest retail analysts would not have predicted that the Big Four would be in the poor shape they are now. But for the time being the idea of a food shop that involves multiple stops and a variety of retailers – the butcher, the baker, a farmers' market – will remain unthinkably inconvenient and unrealistic to many. So perhaps what we need are reinventions of last century's shopping model, like hiSbe, a prototype for a more progressive style of supermarket that can co-exist harmoniously alongside Britain's increasingly dynamic alternative food economy.

5 June 2015

⇨ The above information is reprinted with kind permission from Sustainable Food Trust. Please visit www.sustainablefoodtrust.org for further information.

New guides for business owners in the dark over competition law

Three-quarters of company bosses don't understand competition rules.

By Rebecca Burn-Callander

Company bosses won't be able to claim ignorance over competition law from today, after an industry watchdog published a series of guides around how to avoid being embroiled in price-fixing, bid-rigging and market-sharing.

The Competition & Markets Authority (CMA) created the materials following research earlier this year, which found that 77% of UK firms did not understand competition law.

The move has been welcomed by the Federation of Small Businesses (FSB), which said that competition law was a "crucial" topic for the nation's small- and medium-sized firms.

"We welcome efforts to help small businesses grasp the law in this area – as the potential fallout of getting it wrong could be severe," said FSB national chairman John Allan.

"Competition law is a crucial part of doing business in the UK and these films are a useful tool to help raise awareness of this complex topic."

Although 55% of the company bosses surveyed by the CMA knew price-fixing was illegal, 27% were unsure whether it was acceptable to agree prices with rivals, 23% thought it was "okay to discuss prospective bids with competing bidders" and 29% were not aware whether bid-rigging was illegal.

The CMA has written an at-a-glance guide to competition law, a series of case studies about firms that have broken the law, and created a series of short films flagging illegal practices, to prevent small firms either becoming a victim of crime or perpetrating one.

There are eight animated films in total, and business owners can test their knowledge with a new quiz.

"We have worked closely with groups representing small businesses to learn more about what they do and don't know about competition law and they told us they need information that is short, simple and easy-to-use," said Alex Chisholm, the CMA's chief executive.

"These new materials explain which behaviours are illegal, and why they cause harm. The victims of anti-competitive activity will often be other businesses, so knowing what illegal behaviour looks like and how to report it can help businesses protect themselves from others which are acting unfairly."

The potential consequences of breaking the law are very serious. In August, Consultant Eye Surgeons Partnership was fined £500,000 by the CMA after it admitted several infringements around price-fixing.

Companies found to be in breach of competition law can be fined up to 10% of global turnover and their directors may be disqualified from managing a company for up to 15 years.

Some breaches may be criminal offences, which can result in individuals being jailed for up to five years.

18 November 2015

⇨ The above information is reprinted with kind permission from *The Telegraph*. Please visit www.telegraph.co.uk for further information.

Corruption remains a major cost for honest companies

30% businesses globally reported losing out on deals to corrupt competitors.

Control Risks, the global business risk consultancy, today publishes its annual survey of business attitudes to corruption, comprising interviews with 824 companies worldwide.

⇨ **Corruption is still a major cost to international business.** 30% of respondents reported losing out on deals to corrupt competitors and 30% say they have decided not to conduct business in specific countries because of the perceived risk of corruption. 41% of respondents reported that the risk of corruption was the primary reason they pulled out of a deal on which they had already spent time and money.

⇨ **Corruption risks continue to deter investors.** 30% say they have decided not to conduct business in specific countries because of the perceived risk of corruption.

⇨ **And corruption is killing deals.** 41% of respondents reported that the risk of corruption was the primary reason they pulled out of a deal on which they had already spent time and money.

⇨ **But the picture is improving.** Companies from countries with tight enforcement report fewer losses than before from corrupt competitors. In 2006, 44% of US companies said they had lost out to corrupt competitors, compared with only 24% in 2015. These figures are echoed for Germany and the UK. 81% of respondents agree that international anti-corruption laws "improve the business environment for everyone".

⇨ **However, there is still more to do.** The survey shows that there are still wide variations in the maturity of company programmes. In the worst case, conventional compliance approaches can increase risk because they lead to a misguided sense of complacency.

Control Risks' survey reveals companies are now more willing to challenge when faced with suspected corruption. 27% of companies said they would complain to a contract awarder if they felt they had lost out due to corruption, compared to just 8% of respondents in 2006. In 2006, only 6.5% of respondents said they would appeal to law-enforcement authorities, compared with 19% in 2015, with 24% of respondents now saying they would try to gather evidence for legal action.

Companies feel that international anti-corruption legislation is improving the business environment. Most respondents felt these laws made it easier for good companies to operate in high-risk markets (55%) and serve as a deterrent for corrupt competitors (63%). This was particularly true of companies in developing markets. 79% of Mexicans agree or strongly agree, as well as 68% of Indonesians, 64% of Brazilians and 53% of Nigerians. In the US, 54% say tough laws make it easier to operate in high-risk markets, while 42% disagree.

However, despite these positive developments, Control Risks' survey suggests companies still need to do more. Third-party risk is still relatively unrecognised. Just 58% of respondents have procedures in place for due diligence assessments of third parties and only 43% have third-party audit rights.

The survey also suggests companies are not setting the right incentives to deter corruption. Respondents cited the fear of negative consequences as the penalty used most commonly to deter corrupt behaviour. On the list of eight deterrents to corruption, in sixth place are company performance criteria that emphasise integrity (along with financial targets). Establishing parity between financial targets and anticorruption targets is vital to ensuring compliance is embedded into companies' culture.

Commenting on the survey's findings, Richard Fenning said:

"Governments and companies across the world are increasingly aware of the importance of countering corruption, with China and Brazil in particular stepping up enforcement in the past year. But still too many good businesses are losing out on opportunities to corrupt competitors, or choosing not to take a risk on an investment or entering a new market in the first place for fear of encountering corrupt practices.

"Companies need to find a balance and do more due diligence early on in any negotiation or market entry planning, to spot the points of light in countries that may otherwise appear as no-go areas.

"Another concern is an overreliance on compliance. Often when organisations have comprehensive compliance processes in place, business leaders treat them as a safety net and don't police ruthlessly enough internally. More than half of the businesses we surveyed hadn't conducted a corruption-related investigation in two years. Given the size and complexity of most organisations this would suggest there is a danger of a false sense of security in compliance departments."

12 October 2015

⇨ The above information is reprinted with kind permission from Control Risks. Please visit www.controlrisks.com for further information.

Half of UK banknotes used to fund shadow economy

Bank of England report reveals that only half of notes in circulation are used legitimately, with remainder linked to drug dealing and prostitution.

By Patrick Collinson and Rupert Jones

At least half of all UK banknotes in circulation are being used for purposes such as drug dealing, prostitution and dodgy business deals, or are being held abroad, according to a Bank of England report.

It said that no more than half of banknotes are being used for legitimate purposes, with the rest used to fund the 'shadow' economy or held overseas.

The so-called shadow economy encompasses a range of illegal activities, from drug dealing, prostitution, smuggling, fraud and human trafficking, plus legitimate activities that are concealed from the authorities, such as 'off-the-books' business deals and cash-in-hand payments for goods and services such as building work where the aim is to escape paying tax.

In an extraordinary admission, the Bank said: "The evidence available indicates that no more than half of Bank of England notes in circulation are likely to be held for use within the domestic economy for legitimate purposes.

"The remainder is likely to be held overseas or for use in the shadow economy. However, given the untraceable nature of cash, it is not possible to determine precisely how much is held in each market."

The shadow economy is estimated to be around 10% of the UK's GDP, although it is reckoned to be half the level of Greece and Italy.

The new Bank report follows earlier studies that have suggested that 11% of UK banknotes in general circulation are contaminated with cocaine.

Criminals and tax evaders will often hoard cash, said the Bank, which added that articles in the media reporting on the seizure of large sums during police raids "suggest the values involved may be sizeable".

But it added that official data suggested that activity in the shadow economy had not seen significant growth over the last few years.

It is not just criminals who are hiding away supplies of cash: the Bank said its research indicated that within the legitimate domestic economy, at least £3 billion was being hoarded by UK citizens. "People may choose to save their money in a safety deposit box, or under the mattress, or even buried in the garden, rather than placing it in a bank account," it added. However, it acknowledged that this may be an underestimate of the true situation.

Figures for how much cash is in circulation per head will also come as a surprise to people used to taking out just £20 or £30 out of a cash machine at a time. The Bank of England said: "There is now the equivalent of around £1,000 in banknotes in circulation for each person in the United Kingdom."

However, the equivalent figures for the US and Australia are higher, at £2,500 and £1,220, respectively.

Predictions about the death of cash as consumers switch to contactless payments are premature, said the Bank. It said that while cash usage will drop, it will be around for many years to come.

The report added: "Over the next few years, consumers are likely to use cash for a smaller proportion of the payments they make. Even so, given consumer preferences and the wider uses of cash, overall demand is likely to remain resilient. Cash is not likely to die out any time soon."

Nevertheless, a few countries are seeing dramatic falls in cash usage. The Bank said people in Sweden can now buy almost anything using alternative payment methods and noted that homeless street vendors there who sell a magazine similar to *The Big Issue* were able to accept payment via a debit or credit card, while it was common for Swedish children to be paid their pocket money electronically.

In the next few years new banknotes for the £5, £10 and £20 denominations will be launched. The notes will be made of a polymer substrate – a cleaner and more durable material – and will incorporate security features that will strengthen their resilience against the threat of counterfeiting.

15 September 2015

⇨ The above information is reprinted with kind permission from *The Guardian*. Please visit www.theguardian.com for further information.

Taxi-hailing service Uber paid just £22,134 corporation tax in UK

Uber insisted it had paid "every penny of tax that is due".

Uber is the latest company to risk public anger after paying just £22,134 corporation tax in the UK last year despite making a £866,302 profit here.

A spokesman for the taxi-hailing service denied it had used any loopholes and insisted it had paid "every penny of tax that is due".

He added: "With corporation tax, past losses offset current and future profits – as is the case with Uber which made losses in the UK in previous years. This is an accounting principle to encourage investment that dates back to Benjamin Disraeli. It is not a loophole.

"We will keep reading about big companies like Uber paying a pittance in tax until politicians get a grip on our maddeningly complex tax code"

It comes one week after Facebook revealed it paid just £4,327 corporation tax in the UK in 2014. A string of multinational firms have been criticised in recent months for taking steps to legally avoid corporation tax.

"Uber is set to launch a service for disabled passengers in London"

TaxPayers' Alliance chief executive Jonathan Isaby said such cases would keep arising until the Government took steps to level the playing field for companies.

"We will keep reading about big companies like Uber paying a pittance in tax until politicians get a grip on our maddeningly complex tax code," he said.

"Uber [paid] just £22,134 corporation tax in the UK last year despite making a £866,302 profit"

"The system for taxing companies was designed decades ago and is now totally unsuitable for the modern, digital economy. It is time for politicians to stop their pointless moralising and fundamentally reform the tax code so all companies can compete on a level playing field."

In other news, Uber is set to launch a service for disabled passengers in London.

The minicab-hailing app said more than 100 of its most experienced drivers have signed up to the uberAssist scheme.

Those needing it can request the service by typing ASSISTUK into the promotion screen on Uber's app.

20 October 2015

⇨ The above information is reprinted with kind permission from *Herald Scotland*. Please visit www.heraldscotland.com for further information.

New criminal offences in clampdown on tax evasion

"If people help a burglar, they are accomplices too. Now it will be the same for those that help tax evaders," explains the Chief Secretary.

Tax evaders and the professionals who enable tax evasion will face tough new sanctions, including two new criminal offences and higher penalties, under a new regime to crack down on offshore evaders the Chief Secretary to the Treasury Danny Alexander announced today (Thursday 19 March 2015).

Building on yesterday's Budget announcement that the Government is introducing a new and tough last chance disclosure facility ahead of the worldwide automatic exchange of financial information coming into effect, which the UK championed, the Chief Secretary is today unveiling plans to:

⇨ introduce a new strict liability criminal offence for offshore evasion – so in the worst cases it's no longer possible to plead ignorance in an attempt to avoid criminal prosecution

⇨ make it a criminal offence for corporates to fail to prevent tax evasion or the facilitation of tax evasion on their watch

⇨ increase the financial penalties faced by evaders – including, for the first time, linking the penalty to value of the asset kept in an offshore bank account

⇨ introduce new civil penalties on those who enable evasion so they will face the same penalty as the tax evader

⇨ publicly name and shame both evaders and those who enable evasion.

Chief Secretary to the Treasury Danny Alexander said:

"I have made a great deal of progress in shutting down those loopholes and clamping down on aggressive avoidance and evasion.

I have authorised over £1 billion of investment in HMRC to ensure they have the tools to do their job. There has been a quadrupling of criminal prosecutions and a dramatic rise in taxes collected.

"But now I am announcing that we are going even further. We're making it a crime if companies fail to put in place measures to stop economic crime happening in their organisations. We're also making sure that the penalties on those that facilitate evasion are large enough to punish and deter.

"Tax evasion is a crime like any other. If people help a burglar, they are accomplices and criminals too. Now it will be the same for those that help tax evaders."

As well as action to crack down on offshore tax evaders through a tough new disclosure scheme, the Budget included new penalties and reporting requirements to tackle persistent tax avoiders.

The Chief Secretary has also today called on the tax and accountancy professional regulatory bodies who police professional standards to maximise their role in setting and enforcing clear standards around enabling and promoting avoidance.

The details on the new evasion regime and avoidance sanctions are outlined in a report published today which sets out the Government's approach to tax avoidance and tax evasion.

The Government will consult on the detail of the new evasion regime.

Over the course of this Parliament, as a result of actions taken to tackle evasion, avoidance and non-compliance, HMRC will have secured £100 billion in additional revenue. This includes more than £31 billion from big businesses, and an extra £1.2 billion from the UK's 6,000 richest people, who each have a net worth of £20 million or more.

19 March 2015

This news article was published under the 2010 to 2015 Conservative and Liberal Democrat Coalition Government.

⇨ The above information is reprinted with kind permission from the HM Treasury and HM Revenue & Customs. Please visit www.gov.uk for further information.

© *Crown copyright 2016*

Share more profit with your workers, Centre for Social Justice tells big business

Big businesses taking advantage of benefit system 'top-ups'.

Big businesses should be encouraged to use their profits to increase workers' wages towards the Living Wage and ease the burden on the taxpayer, says a major think tank.

The report by the Centre for Social Justice (CSJ) says businesses have benefitted from sacrifices made by hard-working employees, and with rising economic prosperity workers should be able to share in more of their company's successes.

The think tank claims some businesses are taking advantage of the benefits system by resisting pay increases in the knowledge that the state will 'top up' the income of the low-paid using Tax Credits.

The findings are set out in a new report, *Tackling Low Pay*. The use of Tax Credits to 'top up' low-paid workers' earnings to ensure a reasonable standard of living 'exploded' under New Labour, rising by 2,400 per cent from £1 billion in 1999/2000 to £24 billion in 2008/09.

To incentivise employers to pay a Living Wage, the report calls on big, profitable companies to disclose in an annual report the measures they are taking to become a Living Wage employer and to help their employees progress.

The report also calls for sizeable increases in the National Minimum Wage, after it lost a considerable amount of value during the recession.

With the economy now strong enough to withstand such a rise, it recommends sizeable above inflation increases in the minimum wage until there is evidence it is harming employment.

The report also says that Universal Credit is an important tool in tackling low pay and helping part-time workers

> The London Living Wage currently stands at £9.15 an hour and the Living Wage outside of London at £7.85. There are currently 1,229 Living Wage employers accredited by the Living Wage Foundation.
>
> The London Living Wage is calculated by combining 60 per cent of the median London income and an assessment of the cost of living in London. Outside of London, the living Wage level is set by the Centre for Research in Social Policy at Loughborough University.

gain more hours of employment. Commenting on the report, the author David Skelton, said:

"In a time of growing profitability and economic success, it is unreasonable to expect the taxpayer to continue topping up low pay when big businesses have the ability to increase wages. The recommendations outlined in this report, if implemented, will go a long way to improving the lives of countless people, without costing jobs.

"Low pay and poverty are often associated with a host of other social problems, including family breakdown, serious personal debt and an endless cycle of social and economic deprivation. These are all problems that prevent families and communities from realising their full potential."

The report reveals that three-quarters of workers are shackled by low pay for life. Only around 25 per cent of low-paid workers 'escape' low pay.

The report also finds that 4.3 million workers in the UK have skills and qualifications exceeding those

needed for their job, suggesting that businesses should help their employees to progress in work.

Former CSJ Director Christian Guy said, "This report should be used by an incoming government to inform the next stage of efforts to make work pay."

To help prevent cycles of deprivation, the report outlines a series of other recommendations, including:

⇨ Firms with an annual turnover of more than £100 million should be expected to state on company letterheads and other marketing documents whether or not they pay the Living Wage.

⇨ Living Wage employers should be expected, within reason, to procure all services from other Living Wage employers.

⇨ The Government should ask the Low Pay Commission (LPC) to recommend ways for the minimum wage to recover its lost value as quickly as possible.

⇨ The power of the LPC should be broadened so that it is

responsible for setting the advisory level of the Living Wage outside London. The LPC should also consider the impact on state welfare payments when setting the National Minimum Wage.

⇨ To allow businesses and public sector bodies to plan, the Living Wage level should be announced at least six months before implementation.

⇨ The Low Pay Commission should be asked to provide an annual assessment of the impact of the Living Wage on employment, labour costs, productivity and other key metrics.

⇨ As the financial situation allows, the government should reduce the Universal Credit taper to 55 per cent and possibly lower and increase the work allowance in order to boost work incentives.

⇨ Where feasible, businesses should look to open up development routes within the organisation for low-paid workers.

16 March 2015

⇨ The above information is reprinted with kind permission from the Centre for Social Justice. Please visit www. centreforsocialjustice.org.uk for further information.

What is the new national living wage? How the April 2016 change could affect you

All you need to know about the change to the minimum wage in April.

By Louise Ridley, Assistant News Editor at The Huffington Post UK

Up to one in three workers in some parts of Britain will receive a pay rise when the new 'national living wage' comes into effect today [Friday], according to a new study.

The new legal requirement – which is effectively a new minimum wage – has been called a "hugely ambitious policy", but some areas will benefit more than others from the new £7.20 an hour rate and adults under a certain age won't get it at all, the Press Association reported.

"Up to one in three workers in some parts of Britain will receive a pay rise when the new 'national living wage' comes into effect"

Here are the facts you need to know:

What is the national living wage?

It is a new compulsory minimum wage premium from the British Government – a new higher legal minimum that employers have to pay their staff.

It applies only to workers over 25, and is £7.20 an hour or around £15,000 a year if you work a 40-hour week.

The national living wage is a significant pay increase for those entitled to it – the previous minimum wage for people over 21 is £6.70 an hour – around £13,900 a year if you work a 40-hour week.

When does it come into force?

From 1 April 2016.

How is it worked out?

The Government's new national minimum wage is calculated based on median earnings – it ensures that everyone is being paid at least 55% of the median or average wage.

The Government also plans to raise this to at least 60% of median earnings by 2020 – meaning a rise to around £9 per hour by 2020.

Is it different to the 'living wage' I've heard about already?

Yes. A group called the Living Wage Foundation has been campaigning for employers to pay a living wage – by which is means a wage that will allow people to afford the cost of living – for 15 years.

This 'living wage', which is voluntarily paid by some companies like HSBC, Google and Transport for London, is calculated based on the cost of living and is higher than the Government's national living wage.

The living wage is £8.25 an hour for people outside of London, and £9.40 an hour for those in London.

How many people will benefit?

Across Britain, one in six employees will be affected by the national living wage, with a total of 4.5 million people having an increase on Friday.

This includes around 1.8 million people earning under £7.20 who will get a direct pay rise, and another 2.6 minimum earning just over £7.20, who the Resolution Foundation assume will get a pay rise to differentiate between them and lower-paid workers.

Will it make a difference where I live?

Torridge in Devon, Rossendale in Lancashire, Woking in Surrey and Castle Point in Essex were named as the areas most likely to benefit.

"The new rate will have less impact in London and the South East, with just 3% of workers in the City set to have a wage rise"

The Resolution Foundation said employers in these areas will see "significant" increases in their wage bill.

The biggest city to benefit is Sheffield, where over a fifth of employees will qualify for the higher wage, the report said.

Torsten Bell, director of the Resolution Foundation, said: "The national living wage is a hugely ambitious policy with the potential to transform Britain's low pay landscape. Up to a third of workers will get a pay rise in national living wage hotspots, ranging from Canvey Island to Eastern Lancashire.

How about in London?

The new rate will have less impact in London and the South East, with just 3% of workers in the City set to have a wage rise on Friday, which the think tank said reinforced the importance of the voluntary living wage of £9.40 an hour in the capital and £8.25 in the rest of the country.

"Britain's new legal wage floor will be felt throughout the country, but its impact will be bigger in some areas than others. Relatively few employees will benefit in high-paying parts of Britain such as the City of London and Camden, reminding us of the need to see more employers sign up to pay the higher voluntary living wage.

Will businesses cope?

Bell says: "Of course pay rises don't come free so employers in some sectors and parts of the country will feel the pressure more than others.

"That's why it's vital that businesses and national, regional and local government make the successful implementation of the new legal minimum a priority."

30 March 2016

⇨ The above information has been reprinted with kind permission from The Huffington Post UK. Please visit www.huffingtonpost.co.uk for further information.

© 2016 AOL (UK) Limited

National Minimum Wage and National Living Wage rates

The hourly rate for the minimum wage depend on your age and whether you're an apprentice.

You must be at least:

⇨ school leaving age to get the National Minimum Wage

⇨ 25 to get the National Living Wage – the minimum wage will still apply for workers aged 24 and under.

Current rates

These rates are for the National Living Wage and the National Minimum Wage from 1 April 2016.

Year	25 and over	21 to 24	18 to 20	Under 18	Apprentice
April 2016 (current rate)	£7.20	£6.70	£5.30	£3.87	£3.30

National Minimum Wage rates change every October. National Living Wage rates change every April.

The 'apprentice' rate is for apprentices aged 16 to 18 and those aged 19 or over who are in their first year. All other apprentices are entitled to the minimum wage for their age.

Previous rates

The following rates were for the National Minimum Wage. The rates were usually updated every October.

Year	21 and over	18 to 20	Under 18	Apprentice
2015	£6.70	£5.30	£3.87	£3.30
2014	£6.50	£5.13	£3.79	£2.73
2013	£6.31	£5.03	£3.72	£2.68
2012	£6.19	£4.98	£3.68	£2.65
2011	£6.08	£4.98	£3.68	£2.60
2010	£5.93	£4.92	£3.64	£2.50

Source: National Minimum Wage and National Living Wage rates GOV.UK, 12 April 2016

Ethics at work

2015 survey of employees in Britain.

By Daniel Johnson

Summary and conclusion

This fourth IBE *British Ethics at Work* report has explored the attitudes and perceptions of British employees of ethical standards and behaviours in their workplace. The results in this report provide insight into the state of business ethics in British organisations in 2015. It has also shown how the view of British employees towards ethics in the workplace has shifted over time.

The findings show that between 2012 and 2015 there has not been a significant shift in the experiences of British employees of ethics at work:

⇨ the practice of honesty is still considered to be prevalent with more than four-fifths of employees saying that honesty is practised always or frequently in their organisation

⇨ a consistent fifth say that they has been aware of misconduct over the previous year

⇨ only half of employees aware of misconduct continue to raise their concerns, and

⇨ only 8% say that they had felt pressured to compromise their organisation's ethical standards.

However, each of the elements of a formal ethics programme is now more prominent than three years ago:

⇨ almost nine in ten say that their organisation has written standards of ethical business conduct, up from slightly less than three-quarters in 2012

⇨ a similar proportion say their organisation offers a means of reporting misconduct confidentially, up from slightly more than two-thirds in 2012

⇨ nearly three-quarters say their organisation has an advice or information helpline, up from approximately six in ten in 2012

⇨ almost four-fifths say their organisation provides ethics training, up from less than two-thirds in 2012.

In 2015, ethics programmes now appear to be well established, and are becoming more embedded in organisations as their awareness amongst employees has increased substantially.

However, in a reversal of previous findings, fewer than two-fifths (39%) are now satisfied with the outcome when they raise their concerns of misconduct. In 2012, 70% were satisfied. This is consistent with the finding that not believing corrective action would be taken was the second most prominent barrier to employees raising concerns. The finding that almost three-quarters of employees in organisations with the most supportive ethical cultures said that they were satisfied with the outcome when they spoke up, does however suggest that individual organisations have a degree of control over this.

There is also evidence to suggest the benefits of formally supporting employees to do the right thing. Organisations which take ethics seriously by providing support to employees through formal ethics programmes and/or a supportive ethical culture experience:

⇨ honesty more frequently in their day-to-day operations,

⇨ misconduct less frequently, and

⇨ less pressure on employees to compromise their standards of ethical conduct.

November 2015

⇨ The above information is reprinted with kind permission from the Institute of Business Ethics. Please visit www.ibe.org.uk for further information.

Key facts

- In 2015, there were 5.4 million businesses in the UK. (page 1)

- In 2015, over 99% of businesses are small or medium sized businesses – employing 0–249 people. (page 1)

- In 2015, 5.1 million (95%) businesses were micro-businesses – employing 0-9 people. Micro-businesses accounted for 33% of employment and 18% of turnover. (page 1)

- There were 351,000 business births and 246,000 business deaths in 2014. (page 1)

- In 2015, there were 5.4 million private sector businesses in the UK, up by 146,000 or 3% since 2014. (page 1)

- In 2015 there were 4.0 million businesses in the service industries, three quarters of all businesses in the UK. The biggest of the service industries in terms of the number of businesses was the professional, scientific and technical industry which accounted for 15% of businesses. The retail sector accounted for 10% of all businesses. (page 1)

- In 2014, 20% of SMEs in the UK were majority led by women. This is two percentage points higher than in 2012 and equates to around 1.1 million SMEs. (page 2)

- In 2013 to 2014, central government spent an unprecedented £11.4 billion with small and medium-sized businesses – those employing 250 employees or less. This is equivalent to 26% of central government spend. (page 3)

- Britain saw a 51% increase in new businesses from 385,741 in 2010 to 581,173 in 2014. This compares to an 11% increase in the US, 7% in Japan, 40% in Germany and 39% in France. (page 5)

- An entrepreneur in the UK can now start a company in the UK in less than five days, compared to the global average of 20. (page 5)

- 88% of graduates have considered freelancing or being self-employed. (page 6)

- In the 2012–13 academic year, universities and higher education institutions supported the creation of more than 3,500 start-ups by their recent graduates. This brought the total of active graduate companies created in the last 13 years to 8,127, employing 15,588 staff, receiving investments totalling £28.5 million and having a combined turnover in 2012–13 of £376 million. (page 7)

- Based on the 20,673 registered students, Tenner was mostly endorsed in the South East, South West, North West, West Midlands and London. Together, these regions accounted for half of all students (64%). (page 10)

- The bank reckons family-owned businesses generated revenues of £540 billion last year and that this figure is set to hit £661 billion by 2018. (page 18)

- According to latest statistics, the business creation rate has risen by 55% since 2000. Yet the proportion of enterprises that have employees has actually fallen from a third to a quarter, while the proportion of those with no employees has risen. This means that a lot of the entrepreneurship 'success' that we hear about is actually represented by a 73% rise in the number of people who have become self-employed. (page 22)

- Estimates suggest up to 25,000 people died and more than 550,000 people were injured, some seriously and permanently, after a gas leak incident at the Union Carbide pesticide plant in Bhopal, India, in 1984. (page 23)

- Toyota, the Japanese car giant, agreed to pay out around $1.1 billion in late 2012 to settle a class action lawsuit stemming from complaints of unintended acceleration in its vehicles. (page 24)

- Although 55% of the company bosses surveyed by the CMA knew price-fixing was illegal, 27% were unsure whether it was acceptable to agree prices with rivals, 23% thought it was "okay to discuss prospective bids with competing bidders" and 29% were not aware whether bid-rigging was illegal. (page 31)

- 27% of companies said they would complain to a contract awarder if they felt they had lost out due to corruption, compared to just 8% of respondents in 2006. In 2006, only 6.5% of respondents said they would appeal to law-enforcement authorities, compared with 19% in 2015, with 24% of respondents now saying they would try to gather evidence for legal action. (page 32)

- In 2014, taxi firm Uber paid just £22,134 corporation tax despite making £866,302 profit. (page 34)

Capitalism

An economic system in which wealth generation is driven by privately-owned enterprises and individuals, rather than the state.

Circular economy

Keeping resources for as long as possible in order to extract maximum value from them, and then reusing or recycling the product (or materials from the product) instead of throwing it away.

Competition law

A law that regulates 'anti-competitive' conduct by companies.

Corporate social responsibility (CSR)

Corporate social responsibility, or CSR, is a concept closely linked to business ethics. It refers to self-regulation by a business or corporation, which is built into their overall business model. Companies which are serious about CSR will conduct their business in an ethical way and in the interests of the wider community (and society at large).

Crowdsourcing/crowdfunding

Funding a project, business or venture by raising multiple small amounts of money from the public. This is usually done via the Internet, and usually offers contributors something in exchange for their donation, e.g. those who donate towards publication of a book, may receive a signed copy and other merchandise.

Entrepreneur

An individual who starts and runs their own business.

Freelancer

People who work for themselves and contract out their services.

Gross Domestic Product (GDP)

The total value of the goods and services produced in a country within a year. This figure is used as a measure of a country's economic performance.

Investment

Investing money into a venture or project in return for profit.

National living wage

The national living wage is now £9.15 an hour for those living in London and £7.85 in the rest of the UK. This is the amount that the Government believes is the minimum people need to be paid in order to achieve a basic standard of living in which all necessities can be paid for.

Private sector

Businesses/economy that is not under state control.

Service industry

A business that provides goods but does not manufacture them, for example catering.

Shadow economy

Illicit economic activity.

Shareholder

Anyone who owns shares in a company or corporation.

SMEs

This stands for small and medium-sized enterprises. It describes any company with fewer than 250 employees.

Tax evasion

Avoidance of paying taxes by individuals or businesses.

Turnover

The total amount of business done in a given time.

Assignments

Brainstorming

⇨ In small groups, discuss what you know about business in the UK.

  • What different types of businesses are there?

  • Why do some people choose to become entrepreneurs?

  • What is business education like in your school?

  • What do the letters SME stand for, in business terms?

Research

⇨ Conduct a survey to find out how many students in your school would consider becoming entrepreneurs and starting their own business when they leave school, instead of going to college or university. Write a report that summarises your findings and include graphs to illustrate your results.

⇨ The recent film *Joy* starring Jennifer Lawrence is about a female entrepreneur who invented the Miracle Mop. Do some research to find out about another famous entrepreneur then create a presentation to share your research with your class.

⇨ Research one of the top 20 oldest family businesses in Britain from page 17 and feedback to your class about what they do and how the company has changed over time.

⇨ According to the article on page 29, it could be the 'end of an empire' for supermarkets. Conduct a survey in your local area to find out where people do their grocery shopping. Summarise your findings using bullet points and graphs.

⇨ Imagine that you have been given £500 to start a business. What would you do? In small groups, plan how you would invest your £500 and then share with the rest of your class. You should carefully consider your start-up costs and expected profits.

Design

⇨ Choose an article from this book and create an illustration to highlight its key themes.

⇨ Read the article *The Tenner Challenge* on page 10. Then, in pairs, design a similar scheme that could run within your school to encourage entrepreneurial activity among students. Write a summary of your scheme and how it will work.

⇨ Imagine that you work for a website that allows people to 'crowdsource' their business ideas. Create a series of web banners and draft a marketing e-mail that you could distribute to raise awareness of your platform.

Oral

⇨ "Universities are the best place to start a business." Discuss this statements in small groups.

⇨ Imagine that you are a father or mother who is trying to persuade their eldest child to become involved in the family business. What would you say to convince them of the benefits of family run businesses? Role play the situation.

⇨ What is 'competition law' and do you think it is fair? Discuss in small groups.

⇨ In groups, stage your own version of the television programme *The Apprentice*.

⇨ "There is one and only one social responsibility of business – to use its resources and engage in activities designed to increase its profit so long as it stays within the rules of the game, which is to say, engages in open and free competition, without deception or fraud." – Milton Friedman, American economist. Discuss this quotation in small groups. Following your discussion, take a vote on whether you agree or disagree with Mr Friedman's analysis.

Reading/writing

⇨ Write a one-paragraph definition of a micro-business.

⇨ Look at the infographic on page 6, then visit the Policy Bee website to find out more about graduate entrepreneurs and their feelings about the support they receive from their universities. Write a short essay summarising your findings.

⇨ Imagine that you have decided to start your own business. Write a blog post exploring the motivation behind your decision.

⇨ Choose one of the illustrations from this book and write 300 words exploring what you think the artist was trying to portray with their image.

⇨ Visit the Institute of Business Ethics website (www. ibe.org.uk) and read their report *Ethics at Work*. Write a summary of the key issues that could be used as an introduction to the report on a secondary website, for example as a press release.

⇨ Make a list of the benefits and risks associated with becoming an entrepreneur. Would you ever consider starting your own business?

⇨ Write a letter to your headteacher, explaining why you think it is important for students to have 'real world' business experience.

Bank of England 33
banking 12–13, 23
business ethics 39
business studies
    and corporate crime 12–13
    research programmes 13

cash economy 33
China
    investment in the UK 26
    numbers of new businesses 5
circular economy
    manufacturing and retail potential for 24–5
competition law 31
corporate responsibility
    business ethics 39
    corporation tax payments 34
    corruption 32
    knowledge of competition law 31
    manufacturing and the circular economy 24–5
    to pay a living wage 36–8
    sustainable practices 25
corporations
    corporate business disasters 23–4
    corporate crime 12–13
    corporate social responsibility programmes 23
    corporate welfare 13
    responsibilities to pay a living wage 36–8
corruption 32
crowdfunding
    downsides to 16
    and entrepreneurial growth 5
    equity crowdfunding 15
    internet-mediated nature of 16
    pre-seeded campaigns 15–16

education
    fostering entrepreneurship in schools 8–9, 11
    graduate entrepreneurs in universities 6–7
entrepreneurs
    categorization of self-employed as 22
    crowdfunding 5, 15
    ethnic minorities as 21
    female-led start-ups 2, 21
    fostering entrepreneurship in education 8–9, 11
    graduate entrepreneurs 6–7
    micropreneurs 4
    motivational factors 20
    necessity-driven businesses 20, 22
    opportunity-driven businesses 20
    start-ups in the UK 5
ethnic minority and women-led (EMW) businesses
    key statistics 21
    support policies for 21

family businesses
    challenges of 19
    global scale of 18
    heritage of 17
    as major businesses 17, 18
    strengths of 18–19

Fiver programme 8–9
funding see also crowdfunding
    cash economy 33
    Chinese investment in the UK 26
    peer-to-peer lending 5
    for the shadow economy 33
    Start Up Loans programme 5
    for start-ups 15

graduate entrepreneurs 6–7

high-growth companies 4–5

large businesses see corporations
law
    business violations of 12–13
    competition law 31
    international anti-corruption laws 32
London Living Wage 36

manufacturing
    business disasters 23–4
    potential for the circular economy 24–5
micro-businesses
    definition of 1
    in the UK 1
micropreneurs 4

national living wage 36–8
national minimum wage 36–7, 38

oil industry 23

peer-to-peer lending 5
pensions
    retirement age and pension pots 14

scandals, corporate
    coverage in business studies courses 12–13
    large corporations 23–4
    Tesco supplier payment strategies 27–8, 29, 30
schools
    Fiver programme 8–9
    fostering entrepreneurship in 8–11
    Tenner Challenge 10–11
shadow economy 33
small and medium sized businesses (SMEs)
    definition of 1
    government spending with 3
    growth trends 4–5
    joint male/female ownership 21
    knowledge of competition law 31
    in the UK 1
start-ups
    female-led 2, 21
    funding for 15
    in the UK 5

supermarkets
    challenge to supermarket model 29–30
    consumer shopping patterns 29
    discount supermarkets 29, 30
    hiSbe (social enterprise supermarket) 30
    Tesco supplier payment strategies 27–8, 29, 30

tax
    corporation tax payments 34
    offshore tax evasion 35
Tenner Challenge 10–11
Tesco
    supplier payment strategies 27–8, 29, 30
United Kingdom
    business statistics 1–2
    Chinese investment in 26
    family businesses 17–18

New Enterprise Allowance 22
    oldest family businesses 17–18
universities
    business schools 13
    and graduate entrepreneurs 6–7

wages
    London Living Wage 36
    national living wage 36–8
    national minimum wage 36–7, 38
    universal credit for shortfalls in 36
women
    female-led start-ups 2, 21
    on FTSE-100 boards 1, 2
    SME business owners 1, 2

Acknowledgements

The publisher is grateful for permission to reproduce the material in this book. While every care has been taken to trace and acknowledge copyright, the publisher tenders its apology for any accidental infringement or where copyright has proved untraceable. The publisher would be pleased to come to a suitable arrangement in any such case with the rightful owner.

Images

All images courtesy of iStock, except page 5 © Yolanda Sun, page 24: Pixabay, page 33 © Images Money and page 34 © Lyle Vincent.

Icon on pages 6, 25 & 41 are made by Freepik from www.flaticon.com

Illustrations

Don Hatcher: pages 3 & 35. Simon Kneebone: pages 19 & 28. Angelo Madrid: pages 16 & 31.

Additional acknowledgements

Editorial on behalf of Independence Educational Publishers by Cara Acred.

With thanks to the Independence team: Mary Chapman, Sandra Dennis, Christina Hughes, Jackie Staines and Jan Sunderland.

Cara Acred

Cambridge

May 2016